Modern
GREEK
Poetry

Translated and edited

by RAE DALVEN

GRANGER BOOKS
MIAMI, FLORIDA

MODERN GREEK POETRY

First Published 1949
Reprinted 1976

PRINTED IN THE UNITED STATES OF AMERICA

DEDICATED TO THE MEMORY OF MY FATHER
from whom I heard my first Greek folk songs

TABLE OF CONTENTS

Page 15 *Acknowledgments*

WILLIAM ROSE BENÉT
    17 *Statement*

MARK VAN DOREN
    18 *Statement*

RAE DALVEN
    23 *The Growth of Modern Greek Poetry*
    43 *The Folk Song: Source of Modern Greek Poetry*

        The Bridge of Arta
        Only for this I grieve for you
        You did not deserve it
        The Witch's Daughter
        The Wedding Song
        Digenis
        The Fall of Constantinople
        The Death of the Klepht
        Kitsos
        Arise, beloved, let us go
        Vampire

VINCENZO KORNAROS
    59 *Erotokritos*

MODERN GREEK POETRY

RHIGAS PHERAIOS
  65 *War Hymn*

YIANNIS VILARAS
  68 *Spring*

ANDREAS CALVOS
  70 *The Lover of his Country*
  74 *To the Sacred Battalion*
  76 *The Ocean*

DIONYSIOS SOLOMOS
  84 *The Destruction of Psara*
  84 *I Walked the Road of the Dawn*
  84 *Temptation*
  85 *To Francesca Frazer*
  85 *Hymn to Liberty*
  88 *The Cretan*
  92 *The Dream*
  93 *Easter Day*
  94 *Maria's Prayer*
  99 *Maria's Dream*

JULIUS TYPALDOS
  101 *The Execution of the Klepht*

ARISTOTELIS VALAORITIS
  103 *Photinos*
  105 *Athanase Diakos*
  108 *Kera Phrosini*
  109 *The Creeping Vine*

GERASIMOS MARKORAS
  111 *Two*

TABLE OF CONTENTS

    112 *Innocent Fears*
    112 *A Dead Maiden's Complaint*
    114 *From "The Spring Night"*

GEORGIOS VIZINOS
    115 *The Dream*
    116 *The Hidden Sorrow*

ALEXANDROS PALLIS
    118 *Girl from Roumely*
    119 *Kanaris*
    120 *Woman from Samos*

KOSTES PALAMAS
    122 *Rose-Fragrance*
    122 *The Fathers*
    123 *The Grave*
    124 *The Twelve Songs of the Gypsy*
             The Arrival
             Love
             The Fair of Kakava
             The Prophet
    129 *The Satyr or the Song of Nudity*
    133 *The Dead Youth*
    134 *Laborers*
    134 *Hymn to Passion*

GEORGIOS DROSSINIS
    141 *Greek Earth*
    142 *The Almond Tree*
    143 *Vespers*

LORENZO MAVILIS
    144 *Lethe*
    145 *Olive Tree*
    145 *In Silence*
    146 *Sweet Death*
    147 *Noble Parentage*

C. P. CAVAFY

- 148 *Awaiting the Barbarians*
- 149 *The City*
- 150 *Walls*
- 150 *Trojans*
- 151 *Satrapy*
- 152 *Ithaca*
- 153 *Ionian Song*
- 154 *God Forsakes Anthony*
- 154 *Return*
- 155 *Very Seldom*
- 155 *Manuel Komninos*
- 156 *For Ammonis Who Died at 29 at 610*
- 156 *Morning Sea*
- 157 *Since Nine O'clock*
- 157 *Body Remember*
- 158 *Of the Ship*
- 158 *One of the Jews (50 A.D.)*

KOSTAS KRYSTALLIS

- 160 *I Would Love to be a Shepherd*
- 160 *To the Imperial Eagle*
- 162 *The Vintage*
- 164 *The Embroidery on the Kerchief*

KOSTES HATZOPOULOS

- 166 *Let the Boat Go . . .*

MILTIADES MALAKASSIS

- 168 *Battarias*
- 170 *Spring Storm*
- 172 *The Forest*
- 173 *Takis Plumis*

YIANNIS GRIPARIS

- 176 *Mount Rhodope*

TABLE OF CONTENTS

    176 *Vestal Virgins*
    178 *Reveille for the Dead*
    179 *Comrades in Death*

PETROS VLASTOS
    181 *To My Mother*
    181 *The Village of Love*

LAMBROS PORPHYRAS
    183 *Lacrimae Rerum*
    184 *The Last Fairy-Tale*
    184 *The Trip*
    185 *Epigram*

ZACHARIAS PAPANDONIOU
    186 *The Prayer of the Humble*
    187 *Serenade at the Window of the Wise Man*
    188 *Sad Sunsets*
    189 *Marigo*
    190 *The Old Shepherd*

APOSTOLOS MELACHRINOS
    192 *Playing the Lyre*
    193 *Magic Refrains*
    194 *It is Raining Again*

NICHOLAS KARVOUNIS
    195 *The Song of the Vanquished*

SOTIRIS SKIPIS
    199 *Sweet Athens*
    200 *You Will Remember Me*

MYRTIOTISSA
    201 *Women of Suli*

ANGELOS SIKELIANOS
    205 *Acheloos (The River-God)*
    206 *The Stygian Oath*

209 *Letter From the Front*
212 *Kleisoura*
215 *Resistance*
216 *March of the Spirit*
219 *The Sacred Way*
222 *Daedalus in Crete*

KOSTAS VARNALIS
224 *The Pains of the Virgin Mary*
225 *Doomed*
226 *The Mother of Christ*
228 *The Ballad of Andrew*
229 *The "Good" People*

MARKOS AVGERIS
234 *Granny Tassia*
235 *Plebeian Song*

NICHOLAS KAZANTZAKIS
236 *The Odyssey*

GALATEA KANZANTZAKIS
246 *Sinner*
247 *The Laborer*

KOSTAS OURANIS
248 *Prayer to God*

KOSTAS KARIOTAKIS
250 *Sleep*
251 *Athens*
252 *Prevesa*
253 *Diakos*
253 *Michael*

GEORGIOS SEFERIS
255 *The Cistern*

TEFCROS ANTHIAS
260 *The Clown*

TABLE OF CONTENTS

    260   *Hands thrust in pockets*
    261   *Epilogue*

JOSEPH ELIYIA
    263   *Our Torah*
    264   *Jesus*
    264   *Militarism*

KASSARIS EMMANUEL
    266   *Dynasty of Chimeras*
    268   *The Haunted Ship*

MICHALIS STASINOPOULOS
    270   *Chess Knight*
    270   *The Young Provincial*

SOPHIA MAVROIDI PAPADAKY
    272   *To a Mother*
    273   *The Little Servant*
    274   *Altar of Liberty*
    276   *Love Song*

NICHOLAS PAPPAS
    277   *Post-War Roll Call*
    279   *Four Years*

RITA BOUMY PAPPAS
    282   *Athens*

YIANNIS SPHAKIANAKIS
    284   *The Song of Freedom and the Sea*

YIANNIS RITSOS
    286   *Song to My Sister*
    288   *Spring Symphony*

NICEPHORUS VRETTAKOS
    292   *Child of the Wind with the Harmonica*
    294   *Elegy on the Grave of a Small Fighter*
    295   *Athens*

　　　　296　*Just One More Spring*
　　　　297　*33 Days*

ODYSSEUS ELYTIS
　　　　303　*The Mad Pomegranate Tree*
　　　　304　*Helen*
　　　　306　*Marina of the Rocks*

BIBLIOGRAPHY OF WORKS CONSULTED
　　　　308

INDEX OF TITLES
　　　　314

INDEX OF POETS
　　　　320

ACKNOWLEDGMENTS

In a very real sense, this anthology is a collective job. I am indebted to a great number of poets and scholars in Athens, Paris and New York:

In May 1947, upon my return to Greece for the fifth time, I consulted with Angelos Sikelianos, Photis Photiades, Nicephorus Vrettakos, Markos Avgeris, Galatea Kazantzakis, Nikos and Rita Boumy Pappas, Kostas Varnalis, George Seferis, Theodore Katsimbalis, the late Michael Rodas, Odysseus Elytis, Myrtiotissa, Yiannis Ritsos, and Yiannis Sphakaniakis. I am especially indebted to the poets, Apostolos Melachrinos, Kassaris Emmanuel, Minas Dimakis and Taki Siomopoulos, who sent me necessary material long after I had returned to New York. Above all, I want to thank the poet, Sophia Mavroidi Papadaky, for criticizing my introduction and making some very valuable suggestions.

In Paris I had discussions with the Greek writers, Nikos Kazantzakis, Helle Alexiou, Emanuel Kriaras; with Professor Seferiades and Professor Mirambel, head of the Neo-Hellenic Department at the Sorbonne, who was kind enough to lend me several important books.

In New York, Mark van Doren, William Rose Benét and Eva Sikelianos were most helpful—indeed this book could not have been completed without them. Allen Tate, Eve

Merriam, Alfred Kreymborg and Aaron Kramer were kind enough to favor this anthology with their approval. Professor Moses Hadas and Nondas Panagopoulos were both helpful in criticizing my introduction.

I am especially grateful to Ellen Lebow who read the book in manuscript and made many helpful revisions. Angelo Seferiades, Demetrios Valakos and Christ Chrisoveryis all gave unstintingly of their time in exciting discussions when any regional idioms in the Greek were obscure to me. I have also been indebted to the late Greek-American research scholar, Michael Politis, who tracked down for me some rare books on Greece. To the editors of various magazines and newspapers, and to many friends, I am most grateful for their generous interest and encouragement. And last but not least, I want to thank my publisher, Joseph Gaer, for his help to me and for his enthusiasm for the work of the poets of modern Greece.

TWO STATEMENTS

WILLIAM ROSE BENÉT:

There is one type of revolution that is a little hard for an American to understand, the struggle for a growing and expanding native language. Our own vernacular expression, as it accretes through the years, easily finds its way into our literature. We have no official national language, that we are commanded to use, though our so-called "diplomacy" may still suffer from certain stiff official phrases.

In Greece, however, the battle between the ancient "purist" tongue imposed by official and kingly decree and the living vernacular language of the people, the lifeblood of Greek poetry and song, has been a real contest. In 1901 "purist" professors and their students paraded through Athens, and the issue of the "demotic" or people's language actually became a political one! Of late years there has been a real tussle as to whether the purist language or the demotic should he used in the schools. Today, though the purist is the official language, the demotic is the language of poetry and prose.

Miss Rae Dalven, editor of the present extraordinary anthology of Greek poetry, tells all about this in her extremely interesting preface. The fight for the people's language has been won, and as she says, "The true heritage of Greece belongs to the people who fought for Greek independence and the people's language . . . But most of all, it belongs to the poets of Greece."

Americans should know more of the living and rushing torrent of modern Greek poetry. And here is a book, at last, that presents adequate translations of the greatest poets of Greece since the days of the demotic songs. It fills a great need, and we are fortunate in having, to present and interpret this poetry for us, a woman who is both American and Greek, an enthusiast who is also a scholar, one who sensitively loves language and can carry over the richness of a great tongue of ancient roots into our own.

The "apparatus" of this book will be found thoroughly satisfactory. The poetry of the five greatest Greek poets: Calvos, Solomos, Palamas, Cavafy, Sikelianos, as well as the rest of the forty-four included, is an expert selection of the best. Nothing here "smells of the lamp"—this is living language, full of the spirit of a civilization which no type of tyranny has ever been able to quell, though the history of Greece, as Miss Dalven spreads it before us, has been a constant struggle for freedom, with the end not yet.

A memorable book is here; an inspiring book in a dark time for humanity; a book generously planned and chosen; a work of translation fashioned as a labor of love. It is this kind of interchange of their most uplifted expression, from one great people to another, which may yet save the world.

MARK VAN DOREN:

That the living Greeks are a great people is amply proved for me by the contents of this volume, which I have seen growing in Rae Dalven's hands since the day, six years ago, when she first brought me some of her translations to read. I admired them then as translations—they were natural and alive, as such things rarely are—but I have learned to admire even more the source from which the poetry in them came. By the living Greeks I mean, of course, not merely our contemporaries on the peninsula and the islands where Homer, Sappho, and Sophocles wrote. I mean all the Greeks who have lived in what for Miss Dalven is modern time—a matter of many painful, difficult, and heroic centuries. I mean the people who have poured forth in unkillable abundance this stream of high-hearted and many-minded verse, this full-voiced fountain to whose shouts and murmurs it seems to me very important that we should listen.

If I had only a few minutes to convince some doubting reader I should probably offer him the following list of poems:

> *The Destruction of Psara* by Dionysios Solomos
> *The Execution of the Klepht* by Julius Typaldos
> *A Dead Maiden's Complaint* by Gerasimos Markoras
> *Trojans* by C. P. Cavafy
> *Marigo* by Zacharias Papandoniou
> *Prayer to God* by Kostas Ouranis
> *Jesus* by Joseph Eliyia
> *Post-War Roll Call* by Nicholas Pappas
> *33 Days* by Nicephorus Vrettakos.

And if he still doubted I would have other lists ready, for this one was chosen, if not at random, at least in the consciousness that it contained none of the demotic songs, neither of the two poems about Maria by Solomos, and nothing by Palamas or Sikelianos. But I do not think that he would still be doubtful. Miss Dalven's book, I am confident, is convincing everywhere.

The Growth of
Modern Greek Poetry

THE GROWTH OF MODERN GREEK POETRY

Modern Greek poetry reflects the indomitable struggle of a people determined to be free. This is manifested as much in the use of their language as in their subject matter. For there are two main currents in modern Greek: the *demotic* or vernacular, for centuries the spoken language of the people; and the *katharevousa* or purist, exclusively based on the Attic of ancient Greece. Both the *katharevousa* and the *demotic* have played important roles in the political as well as the cultural and social lives of the people. Whenever there has been a democratic form of government, the *demotic* was officially taught in the schools and used in the courts of the land; whenever the controls of government fell into the hands of the monarchists, the purist became the official language of school and law. In 1949, the official language of Greece was the purist or *katharevousa,* while modern Greek poetry, as well as all other creative writing, appears mainly in the *demotic,* the language of the people.

My selection of material for this anthology, has, however, not been influenced by a poet's use of language, demotic or purist.

All the great poets of modern Greece have been nourished from childhood on the demotic songs. These demotic songs have come down to the Greek people through the ages by word of mouth. They were created anonymously on all themes concerning the daily lives of the people and especially cultivated by the fighters against oppression.

We know that the ancients improvised anonymous songs about birth, marriage, death, magic, sacrifice, oracles, enigmas. They created rhythmic songs to lighten the burden of their labors: carding the wool, spinning, weaving, pressing the olives, hauling in their fishnets, harvesting the crops. This oral tradition of the ancients is still alive in Greece today. On St. John's Day, teen-agers celebrate on the streets by leaping over fires and spontaneously improvising distichs. Constantine Psachos, Professor of Byzantine Music at the Conservatory of Athens related once that while traveling in the north of Greece, he was inspired by the merriment of a friendly gathering to compose a demotic poem in the tradition of the ancients. This he passed off as "anonymous." Shortly afterwards, he heard his "anonymous" song, sung by the people of the Peloponnese.

Thus it is not surprising to find most Greek villagers with a large repertory of these demotic songs. Recently, a democrat exiled to Icaria, separated from all his books, compiled a collection of demotic songs entirely from memory! Today the people of Greece sing the demotic songs at baptisms, at marriages, on religious holidays, name days and Saints' Days. They sing and dance to these songs often with no instrumental accompaniment at local fairs where they gather from surrounding villages to honor their patron saints. These people's songs and dances are the most significant social outlet of the Greek people from the severity of their labors, the stern struggle for their survival. "The Greeks are a people who feel more keenly than any other the strength of the song," says the poet Apostolos Melachrinos in the introduction of his book *Demotic Songs*. He goes on to say, "The song like a magic power has kept the Greek people a nation for three thousand years."

Certain groups of these demotic songs have come to be identified with different regions. There are Cretan songs, songs of Mani (near ancient Sparta), songs of Roumely, Epirus, Pelion. Each region has its own idiom, its own traditions, but all of them are united by the common theme: the struggle of the Greek people for their liberation.

The creative life of a nation is best expressed through the spoken language of its people. Through the spoken language a people can best defend its democratic rights. There are Greeks however who do not believe in the independence of their own people. These Greeks maintain that the demotic is a degenerate form instead of a development of the ancient Attic. As inheritors of ancient Greece and the Byzantine Empire, they have betrayed the great democratic tradition of that heritage by trying to force upon the people the purist—an artificial imitation of a language spoken two thousand years ago!

The poets of modern Greece who feel the creative bond which exists between a people and their spoken language use a vocabulary which has been proven by time to serve the needs of the people. They even use words from other modern languages often based on the ancient Greek. They feel it would be false to coin new words arbitrarily when the people can apply words already in use. They think it equally false to burden the living language with outmoded forms and meanings—as false as it would be for Americans to speak or write in the language of Chaucer.

From the fourth century B.C. to the eighth century A.D. the accepted language of the Greek people was the Attic which, because of the political leadership of Athens and the greatness of her literature, superseded all other forms of ancient Greek.

The conquests of Alexander the Great (365-323 B.C.) caused the Attic to be adopted as the language of his empire which extended over three continents. In time, words of other languages were assimilated and Alexander was obliged to modify the Attic. This modified Attic is called the common language or *koine* and is sometimes called Hellenistic Greek. There are differences in pronounciation, grammatic construction and the meanings of words, but on the whole it is modeled on the Attic. The Greek of the *Septuagint* and *The New Testament* are written in the *koine*, which has served as a transition from the Attic to the language spoken in Greece today. In his essay *Modern Versus Ancient Greek* the demoticist Petros Vlastos states, "it is now admitted that Greek from the days of Homer to the Klephtic ballads constitutes an unbroken language evolving slowly through thirty centuries of crowded history. Whoever wants to know it thoroughly must become familiar with all its phases."

It is not the purpose of this essay to trace the inflections and changes from ancient to modern Greek. However it is important to note here those elements in the demotic which the purists despise. The demotic has tenaciously preserved the merits of the Attic and the ancient *koine* but ruthlessly dropped all cumbersome construction and forms. In addition and just as tenaciously the demotic has clung to the vocabulary and idiomatic expressions gained through two thousand years of contact with Italian, Slavonic, Albanian, Turkish, French and other western languages. The purists are battling to strip modern Greek of its melodic simplicity and its enriched language won by the people in their historic struggle to liberate themselves from their own heritage as well as from the rest of the western world.

With the establishment of Christianity, language became an open issue. The conservative clergy delivered their homilies in the purist Attic. There was a wide gap between the purist

THE GROWTH OF MODERN GREEK POETRY

literary language and the spoken language. The lay clergy and the people spoke in the vernacular.

In the eighth century, St. John of Damascus (700-754) organized liturgical songs and wrote *troparia*, ecclesiastical verses set to ancient melodies. St. John of Damascus also wrote a novel in the vernacular entitled *Barlaam and Ioaseph* which has been translated into many languages. The hymn-wright Romanos wrote hymns glorifying every event around the birth of Christ. He wrote *troparia* to the Virgin which the people sang to celebrate their victory against the Arabs early in the ninth century.

A song written in the vernacular which has come down to us from this period, is the *Song of Armouri* or *Armouropoulos* written as a tribute to Michael III (839-867) who was murdered by the "Macedonian" Basil the First (812-886) because Michael preferred the people's language and defended the social and universal aspects of Christianity. This *Song of Armouri* belongs to the cycle of Digenis Akritas (leader who fought to liberate the people), the outstanding contribution of Byzantium to the vernacular. The Akritan epics are about the men who aided Digenis.

Beside the legend of Digenis Akritas, the Byzantine Era produced *The Song of Spaneas* attributed to Alexis Komnenos (1081-1118) an admonitory poem in the vernacular. The Byzantine Era also produced the poems in the vernacular of the scholarly monk Theodore Prodromos (twelfth century) better known as Ptochoprodromus. He is the first author to have written poems in the demotic. He wrote a poem addressed to the Emperor Manuel Komnenos (1143-1180) to complain of the impoverished state of men of letters.

From the twelfth century on we find more and more verse written in the vernacular. Rhymed romances began to appear at this time, inspired chiefly by the chivalry of the Frankish invaders (1204) and written mainly to combat the efforts of the "purists" whose eyes still turned retrogressively to the past. The occupation of southern Greece in the thirteenth century by the Franks inspired the *Chronicle of the Conquest of Morea,* a medieval history in verse of the feudal prinicipalities in the Peloponnese. *The Chronicle of Machaira* was also written at this time. But the masterpiece of the fourteenth century is *Belthandros and Chrystanza,* which some critics consider to be superior in imaginative power to the *Niebelungenlied.*

The fall of Constantinople in 1453 marked the collapse of Byzantium and the beginning of four centuries of Turkish domination. The Patriarch of Constantinople was made an official of the Turkish Empire and the head of a half-independent Christian state. The sultan granted privileges to the Phanariot aristocracy, so-called from Phanari, seat of the Patriarchate. In many cases, the Phanariots were appointed governors of the large provinces of the Turkish Empire. The Phanariots and the higher clergy tried to restore the "purist" in imitation of the Attic, although their spoken language was the demotic.

Through the remaining years of the fifteenth century under Turkish domination, the Greek people started no national movement for their liberation. In the sixteenth century, a group of men arose to preserve the Greek vernacular. Nikolaos Sophianos, born in Corfu, felt that it would be impossible to educate the common people unless something were done to weaken the conservative ecclesiastical tradition of the Attic. In 1542 he translated into the vernacular Plutarch's *Concerning Child Education.* He wrote a grammar in the vernacular but this did not appear in print until 1870. Towards the end of the sixteenth century, Maximos Margounios, Bishop of the island of Cythera and Meletios Pygas, Patriarch of Alexandria, delivered their sermons in the vernacular. Cyril Loukaris (1572-1638) Patriarch of Constantinople in 1621 had the first printing press brought to the capital. He fought a lively though unsuccessful battle against the conservatives who opposed his desire to translate the Bible into the vernacular. He was suspected of Protestantism by his enemies and ultimately calumniated by the Jesuits to the Sultan who put him to death on a charge of instigating rebellion.

In the 17th century, the Greek merchants and shipowners had grown sufficiently strong to revolt against the feudal economy. They started Greek schools in secret and led in the demotic movement. In 1638 Simon Porkios, born in Crete, a doctor of theology in Rome, published a *Grammar of the Greek Vernacular*. Elias Miniatis (1669-1714) eminent Greek clergyman wrote a book entitled *Teachings* (printed in Venice in 1728) which contains many of the sermons which he delivered in the vernacular. In 1681 Francis Skoufos, a clergyman inspired by his hatred of the Turks, wrote a book in the vernacular entitled *Rhetoric*. At this time too, the Cretans renowned for their leadership and revolt during the Venetian domination (1204-1669) led in the movement to preserve the spoken language and were actually responsible for a renaissance in Greek letters.

Four outstanding literary works in the demotic were written by Cretans during the Turkish domination: *Abraham's Sacrifice* was first published in 1534. *Gyparis,* a pastoral tragicomedy was written anonymously about 1600. *Erophile* was first published in Venice in 1637 after the death of the author, George Hortatsis, who had written it in the spoken Greek with Italian characters. But the best known work of Venetian Crete is *Erotokritos*, a romantic poem written about 1650 by Vincenzo Kornaros and published for the first time in 1713 in Venice. When the Venetians lost the island of Crete to the Turks in 1669, the Cretan period came to an end. The cause of the vernacular was later championed by the Ionian poets who founded the Ionian School of Demotic Poetry.

The conservative elements of the new merchant class felt that the demotic was deficient in technical terminology and was not meeting their needs. Adamantios Koraes (1748-1833), regarded as the greatest educator by the Greek people, thought he had found a way to meet this need. Koraes, who had done much to spread the western practices of the church, was deeply inspired by the democratic ideals of the French Revolution and sought to spread these ideals among the Greek people. But he failed to see the struggle of the demotic as part of the struggle for liberation. He thought the demotic language was "corrupted" by "foreign words" and "degenerate formations." He recommended a "middle road" which would oust foreign words and put in their place the technical and scientific terminology of the ancient language. The merchant class who needed the immediate support of all the people to carry out their plans for Greek liberation, could not wait for the illiterate masses to be educated in the "middle road" of Koraes. This inability of the otherwise democratic minded educator to accept the spoken idiom was directly responsible for the demotic movement which slowly gathered its forces to make the vernacular the official language of Greece.

The Greeks living in various parts not under Turkish domination such as Crete, Rhodes, Cyprus, Chios, the Morea and the Ionian Islands, began a militant struggle to free the nation from the Turks. They joined forces with the klephts (thieves), first looked upon as mountain bandits of the Robin Hood type who stole from the rich to give to the poor. Later, the klephts lived in open rebellion against the Turks down to the time of the Greek Revolution in 1821 when they became the vanguard in the struggle for Greek Independence. They had *limeria* (areas under their rule), where they held their councils and feasts in the Peloponnese, Olympos, Pelion, Pindos, Agrapha and others. The guerrillas today are following in the tradition of the klephts.

The ideas of the American War of Independence and the French Revolution were rapidly disseminated throughout Greece. A group of forward looking educators arose who tried to bring about a sensible standardization of the vernacular. Men of letters wrote stirring poems of freedom in the demotic.

The first national poet of modern Greece and the first martyr of the Greek War of Independence of 1821 was Rhigas Pheraios (1751-1798) also known as Rhigas Velestinlis. He wrote a Constitution based on the principles of the French Revolution and the Rights of Man. His goal was to overthrow the feudal regime and reorganize the Turkish Empire on a democratic basis with full equality of all peoples and creeds. He cultivated friendships with the Serbs, Rumanians, Bulgarians. He wrote fiery songs of freedom, some of which are still sung in Greece today.

Rhigas spread the idea of Balkan unity through Moldo-Vlachia or Rumania, center of Greek feudal lords, intellectuals and merchants from Phanari, the seat of the Greek Patriarchate in Constantinople. He then went to Vienna, chief Hellenic center outside of Greece proper where the first Greek newspaper was established in 1793 and succeeded in spreading his ideas for Greek liberation there. In 1796, at Leipzig, he had his revolutionary ideas printed in pamphlet form, illustrated with maps and shipped to Trieste. There he hoped to pick them up and take them back himself to Greece where they would be distributed among the people. The Austrian police, allies of the Turks, discovered the pamphlets and when Rhigas arrived at Trieste they seized him and turned him over to the Turks. The Turks transferred him to Belgrade where he was strangled to death in June 1798, the year Dionysios Solomos was born. It is said that Rhigas's last words were, "I have sown enough seed. My people will gather its fruit."

The death of Rhigas was a great loss to the people preparing to fight for their independence. They were surrounded by enemies at home and abroad. Within Greece, the titled Phanariots, eager to retain the privileges granted them by the Turks, were against the idea of revolution. The higher clergy had consistently undermined national feeling all through the years of Turkish enslavement. Men like Koraes who represented the middle-class insisted that the time for revolution had not yet come.

Individual philhellenes of other nations sympathized with the Greek people and some, like Lord Byron, dedicated their lives to the cause of Greek independence. But in the beginning, no nation was moved to help liberate the Greek people. General John Makriyiannis (1797-1864) a man of the people who had never studied the demotic but who spoke it with all the richness of the folk idiom, taught himself how to write the vernacular phonetically and wrote vividly in his memoirs of the period. "The Europeans disparaged the unfortunate Greeks. England wanted them to become Englishmen, in keeping with the English justice prevailing, like the barefooted and hungry Maltese; the French wanted them to become Frenchmen; Russia wanted them to become Russians and Austria wanted them to become Austrians. And whichever of the four could, would devour them."

It was thus left to the common people to liberate themselves. The new bourgeoisie, the secular clergy, the peasants, fishermen, shepherds, were joined by the klephts in an uprising against the Turks. They were joined too by the democratic minded sons of the aristocracy and the Ionian poets who had turned away from their Italianate background and embraced with zest the demotic songs.

Outside of Greece, the Society of Friends (Filike Etaireia), secret popular organization for Greek Independence was established in 1816 in Odessa to enlist the support of other nations and integrate the various Greek communities scattered throughout the world. A month before the war broke out in

1821, Prince Alexander Ypsilante, a General of Greek birth in the Russian Army, disobeyed the Czar's orders not to interfere in the cause of the Greeks and proceeded to Bucharest at the head of a battalion of 300 students. Ypsilante's incompetence and inability to enlist the support of the agrarian populations ended the revolt in Rumania in complete failure. Andreas Calvos wrote about this student battalion in his poem entitled *To A Sacred Battalion*, which is included in this collection. On March 23, 1821, Karatsas, an active member of the Society of Friends started the revolt of Patras and on March 25, the daring and courageous priest Papaflessas convinced the hesitant Bishop Germanos of Patras to raise the Greek flag which began the war against Turkey.

In 1814, the poet Yiannis Vilaras (1771-1823) of Epirus published a Greek grammar at Corfu entitled *The Greek Vernacular*. In this book Vilaras used a new spelling and he defended the spoken idiom as the only possible language for literary expression. The book greatly influenced the poets Dionysios Solomos and Valaoritis and foreshadowed the whole demotic revolt which broke loose in all its fury with Psihari's publication in 1888 of *The Voyage*, written in the vernacular.

When the diplomat and historian Spiridon Tricupis went to visit Dionysios Solomos in 1822, he convinced the Italian educated poet to turn to the Greek language he had imbibed "with his mother's milk." Solomos, regarded today as the national poet of Greece, took his advice, turned his attention to the demotic and from then on dedicated himself to the two causes: Liberty and language. In 1824, Solomos wrote his *Hymn to Liberty* which became the national anthem of Greece. The same year there appeared in France, Fauriel's *Chants Populaires de la Grece Moderne*. Solomos read Fauriel's Introduction whose opinions on the Greek vernacular confirmed the poet's own feelings about the spoken language. In *The Dialogue,* an impassioned and witty conversation between a poet and a pedant, Solomos (the poet), ridiculed the pedants for the artificiality of their speech.

The demotic songs of this period played an important part in preparing the people for the Greek War of Independence and kept up their spirits during the trying eight years of warfare. Some of these klephtic songs were created around Theodore Kolokotrones (1770-1843) the "old man of Morea" under whose leadership the Greeks fought successfully against the Turks. Some klephtic songs were also written about Athanasios Diakos, the deacon who fought as kelpht and led a heroic battle in Alamana near Thermopylae. Diakos was captured by the Turks who roasted him on a spit. Legend has it that he kept on singing until he died.

In the struggle to establish the demotic as the official language of Greece, Solomos was supported by such poets as Aristotelis Valaoritis (1824-1879), Julius Typaldos (1814-1883) Gerasimos Markoras (1826-1911) and Jacob Polylas (1824-1896) editor of Solomos's works. Solomos was opposed by the "purists" and Adamantios Koraes who persisted in a "middle road" for the demotic.

In 1849 the demoticists suffered a serious setback when King Otto, the first king of Greece since its independence from Turkey, established the "purist" as the official language. The cumbersome idiom was taught in all schools. Its lifeless grammatical forms filled all documents. From 1849 to the end of the nineteenth century the "purist" remained the official language of Greece. Newspapers were written in the "purist;" it was taught in the schools. The lively sources of the vernacular were disregarded in this backward look toward ancient Greece.

In the last two decades of the 19th century a healthy realism began to combat successfully the pseudo-romanticism of the purists. A group of demoticists led by Kostes Palamas (1859-1943) met every Saturday night at his home to make plans to strengthen the cause of the demotic which they considered the only hope for the future of Greece. There was the patriot poet and sonneteer Lorenzo Mavilis (1860-1912). It is said that once Mavilis argued with a pedant about the vernacular. When the purist called the demotic a vulgar language, Mavilis replied: "A language can never be vulgar, only people can be vulgar." There was Petros Vlastos (1879-1941) who had simplified the spelling and grammar of the demotic. There was Georgios Drossinis (1859-) very active as editor-in-chief of the magazine *Estia* which supported for twelve years the cause of writers who wrote in the demotic. Angelos Sikelianos (1884-) only a boy at the time was also to be seen at these meetings.

The work of these poets and others who wrote in the demotic also appeared in *Noumas* a magazine founded by Demetrius Tangopoulos (1867-1936) and edited by him from 1903-1925, afterwards continued by his son Panos Tangopoulos until his death in 1931.

Photis Photiades (1849-1939) in Constantinople strengthened the cause of the demotic. Corresponding with his son in Athens who wrote to his father in the purist, Photiades realized how false this language sounded. He wrote a series of articles in the Greek newspaper at Constantinople in defense of the vernacular and a book on the demotic called *Our Language*.

In 1888 Yiannis Psiharis (1854-1929) wrote *The Voyage* in which he ridiculed the purist and argued an uncompromising adoption of the vernacular as the only hope for Greek literature and for the common people. Nicolas Politis (1852-1921) gathered material for his important collection of demotic songs. Alexandros Pallis (1851-1941) translated *The New Testament* and *The Iliad* into the vernacular.

In the theatre, there were presentations of pastorals in the demotic, such as *Golfo* and *The Shepherd's Sweetheart*. Gregory Xenopoulos (1867-) gained wide popularity through his satirical comedies on Athenian life and his novels dealing with social problems.

The counter struggle of the purists was led by the satirist Alexandros Soutsos, (1803-1863) and his brother the lyric poet Panajotis Soutsos (1805-1869), the epic poet Theodorus Orphanides (1817-1886) the famous botanist Alexandros Rizos Rangavis (1809-1892), Demetrios Paparragopoulos (1843-1873) Spiridon Vasiliados (1844-1874) and others.

In the introduction to the translation of Palamas's *Life Immovable*, Prof. Phoutrides reports that in 1901 there were "Gospel Riots" which caused bloodshed on the streets of Athens because Alexander Pallis's translation of *The New Testament* appeared serially in the daily newspaper *Akropolis*. The purists headed by Professors Mistriotis and Hadjidakis, both teaching at the University of Athens, aroused their students to parade wildly through the streets of Athens. They broke down the establishment of the newspaper *Akropolis* where Pallis's *The New Testament* had been printed, and entreated the Archbishop of Athens to excommunicate all the "hairy ones" as the demoticists were labeled by purists. The Archbishop refused the demands of the purists. This refusal made them so violent that arms had to be used against them. Purists used the demotic issue to further their own political ambitions. When they were unsuccessful, they caused the cabinet to resign, the Archbishop to abdicate and to be sent in exile to a monastary in Salamis. Two years later, another riot broke out because of the presentation in the vernacular of the trilogy of Aeschylus. This time too, arms had to be used to curb the riot, and one innocent passerby was killed.

In 1908, unrecognized by the State, Saratsis, director of a

school in Volo, established the vernacular in his educational program. Though the government ordered the school closed, the brilliant results achieved were a blow to the purists. In 1910 at Nauplia, a group of purists brought the demoticists to court on the charge that they were corrupting the faith and tradition of the Greek people. The demoticists won this trial and the victory was another blow to the purists. In that year Nicolas Politis's outstanding collection of *Our Demotic Songs* appeared. The lyric poet Zacharias Papandoniou wrote a new reader in the vernacular which he called *High Mountains*. This book changed the whole approach to the teaching of Greek in the first four years of the public school. In 1911 a military revolution developed the liberal movement which spread under the leadership of the statesman Eleftherios Venizelos (1864-1936). Venizelos and his main advisor Demetrios Glinos (1822-1945), at that time director of the Ministry of Education, not only organized the demotic language in the first four grades of the public school but were instrumental in establishing the demotic language classes of the higher grades.

From 1910 to 1925 a brilliant group of educators fought to make the demotic the official language of the schools. Ably organized by Demetrios Glinos, Manolis Triantaphylides (1883-), Alexandros Delmouzos (1880-) and others, they defended the cause of the vernacular in thirteen volumes of memoranda, bulletins, handbooks and readers and succeeded in making the vernacular the official language in the public schools, secondary schools and even normal schools. In 1917, the demotic was finally recognized as the official language by the State. It was taught in the first six years of the public school. The purist continued to be taught along with the vernacular, in the last two years.

In 1927, the Delphic Idea of Angelos Sikelianos and his American wife Eva Palmer gave the demotic cause a virile and concrete expression at Delphi. The long-range objective of the Delphic Idea was to establish a University on the site of the meeting of the Amphictyonic Council (an ancient congress of confederated states). The greatest arts of Greece and of all nations were to be brought together in periodic festivals. Later, year-round courses were to be established in all the arts, sciences, handicrafts and athletics.

Eva Palmer directed *Prometheus Bound* and *The Suppliants* of Aeschylus both translated into the demotic by the poet Yiannis Griparis. These she presented in 1927 and 1930 in the ancient theatre at Delphi with traditional modal music in the tragic choruses, the singing and dancing performed by non-professional Athenian girls. Ancient and contemporary athletic games were presented in the stadium. Peasants came to Delphi from all the provinces to display their varied handicrafts in the houses of the near-by village of Kastri. They danced their own local dances on the threshing floors (original Greek theatre) in the interludes between the principal events, while crowds of spectators watched, fascinated by the naturalness, the spontaneity and high artistic level of the common people of Greece. The first festival, which lasted one day, was a synthesis of the demotic spirit which had been struggling to survive for centuries.

In 1932 the purists ousted the vernacular from the schools. Undaunted, the demoticists continued their fight and several years later the spoken language was reinstated in public schools.

During the dictatorship of Metaxas (1936-1940) the demotic was championed for propaganda purposes. Metaxas allowed presentations in the vernacular of Pericles' *Funeral Oration,* Sophocles' *Antigone,* and Lincoln's *Gettysburg Address.* But he made certain that all passages against tyranny and dictatorship had been deleted.

During the Nazi occupation the schools followed the Metaxas path but then introduced new "purist" books. In the fall of 1944, "The Government of National Unity" as it was known, decreed that the demotic become the official language of Greece. In 1945, however, the royalist Voulgaris government rescinded the decree and restored the "purist" as the official language. More recently a production of Shakespeare's *Julius Caesar* was denied production because of its passages against tyranny.

Since the occupation the purist has become the official language of the schools. From the third to the sixth grade, reading books contain a pedantic hybrid. Young children mix the two without being able to learn either. In the high schools science and mathematics books are all written in the purist. Only in readers is it compulsory to have some literary selections in the vernacular. In composition, the purist is in order. A student who writes his high school entrance examinations in the demotic risks failure.

Though the purist is the official language of the State today, and purists continue their fanatic attack on the demotic, the spoken idiom predominates in poetry and prose. Scientific books have begun to appear in the vernacular, though this is the only field in which the terminology remains purist. In 1938, Photis Photiades wrote the first medical book in the demotic. Ellisaos Yiannides has written two school text books in the demotic, one on geometry and one on astronomy. Heralambos Theodorides has written an *Introduction to Philosophy* in the vernacular. All documents issued by the Greek Liberation Front (EAM) including the White Book (1945) are worded in the demotic. All the decrees of the PEFA, People's Councils and People's Courts, of the liberated areas during the Nazi occupation as well as most of the official agreements among the various organizations of the resistance were written in the demotic. Yet purists still look upon the spoken idiom as a "vulgar tongue" which violates the heritage of Greece.

The true heritage of Greece, however, belongs to those Greeks who are consciously striving to foster the creative genius of the nation. It belongs to the men and women of the "Educational Group" who labored painstakingly to place the people's idiom back upon the cultural base from which purists have tried to remove it. It belongs to men like Rhigas Pharaios who symbolizes Greece today no less than he did in 1790. But most of all it belongs to the poets of Greece from ancient times to the present who used the demotic as the language of their poetry, and by so doing have kept alive in the hearts of the people the song which has helped to preserve them as a nation these past three thousand years.

THE FOLK SONG: Source of
Modern Greek Poetry

THE FOLK SONG: Source of Modern Greek Poetry

The Bridge of Arta *refers to the bridge that spans the Arta River and dates back to the Roman period (146 B.C.-710 A.D.). The Bridge of Arta is a great favorite and is sung not only all over Greece, but in the neighboring countries as well:*

THE BRIDGE OF ARTA

Forty-five artisans and sixty apprentices
worked for three years on Arta's bridge.
Each day they built and each night it fell in ruins.
The artisans lamented, the apprentices wept:
"Woe to our efforts, our fruitless labours,
all day long we build; at night the bridge falls!"
And a ghostly voice replied from the span upon the right:
"Unless a human life is given, the wall will never stand!
Nor must you sacrifice an orphan, a stranger or a passerby,
only the lovely wife of the master builder,
she who comes late in the morning, who comes late at
[noon. . ."
The master builder heard and was saddened unto death;
he framed a message and sent it to her by the nightingale:
"Make ready slowly, dress slowly, come late in the afternoon,
slowly walk to Arta's bridge and slowly walk across it."

But the bird heeded not and delivered another message:
"Make ready quickly, dress quickly, come quickly at noon,
quickly walk across the bridge of Arta."

Soon she came walking down the white road;
the master builder saw her and his heart broke within him.
"Health and joy to you, artisans and to you apprentices!
But what ails the master builder to make him look so grim?"

"His ring has fallen and is lost in the shaft,
and who will go down, who will enter to look for it!"

"Builders, do not fret, I will go and fetch it,
I will go down and I will enter to find the ring."
She was not all the way down, not even half way down:
"Pull me up, my good man, pull me up," she cried,
"I have searched everywhere and found nothing."

One spread the mortar, one smoothed with the trowel,
the head artisan lifted and heaved a huge stone.

"Alas for our fate, for our pitiless destined end!
We were three sisters and the three evil-fated,
one spanned the Danube, the other Avlona,
and I, the last of all, the bridge of Arta.
As my heart quakes, may the bridge quake,
as my hair falls, may those who pass fall!"

"Mistress, unsay your words, pronounce some other curse,
you have an only brother, who may cross over! . . ."

So she unsaid her words, pronounced another curse:
"May my heart be iron, may the bridge be iron,
may my hair be iron and may those who pass be iron,
for I have a brother in foreign lands who may cross over."

The dirge was widely used in ancient Greece and we find many laments in the classics. In The Iliad *there is a lament*

THE FOLK SONG: SOURCE OF MODERN GREEK POETRY

sung by Achilles on the death of his friend Patroclus. Again in The Iliad *a lament is sung for Hector whom Achilles had killed. Bion, the bucolic poet, wrote* A Lament for Adonis. *Moschos wrote a* Lament for Bion. *Dirges continued to be sung during the Byzantine Era and during the four centuries of Turkish domination. Kostes Palamas followed this tradition in his poem* The Grave, *which he wrote in 1897 on the death of his seven-year-old son, Alkis. An excerpt from this poem appears in this book.*

Keening was left to the women in ancient Greece, just as it is today, and professional women mourners are still hired to extol the departed. Often the Greek "mirologi" or dirge is composed extemporaneously by the nearest relative. When a professional mourner is hired, she leads the chant of the "mirologi." Other women join her, and they end their "mirologi" in a piercing wail.

The two laments which follow are sung in Greece to mourn the loss of a young person:

Only for this I grieve for you, I pity you,
how will you live your first night in the earth?
You will find snakes embraced, vipers entwined.
A snake, a black snake, a two-headed snake,
has nested on your joined brows.

Another lament of a similar nature is often chanted:

You did not deserve it, a bed in the earth was not for you,
you belong in the garden of May,
between two apple trees, under three bitter orange trees,
blossoms gently falling, the apples on your lap,
carnations a red circlet round your neck.

In the few allusions to magic in the literature of ancient Greece, the agents of magic were generally women. The Pythian priestesses at Delphi held oracular powers. Medea, the "wise woman," possessed a terrifying knowledge of herbs and charms which she used for evil purposes. Circe turned Odysseus's men to swine. Athene worked magic on Odysseus himself. Theocritus wrote one of his idylls, "Incantation" about a woman preparing magic charms to bring back her faithless lover. But magic was not left to the women alone, nor was it used for evil purposes only. Asclepios, the god of Health, effected his cures by dreams and spells at his sanctuary in Epidaurus.

In modern Greece, wherever people are still isolated from western ideas, the subject of witchcraft is particularly absorbing. This is especially true at times when the women gather together in the houses of their neighbors for a cup of Turkish coffee and a bit of gossip. Once the coffee is sipped, the coffee cup is turned over on the saucer into which the thick coffee powder at the bottom slowly settles in patterns. These are "read" by the villagers to explain the baffling mysteries of life and death. Sometimes a woman in despair over some obstacle to happiness resorts to melting a chunk of lead which she pours sizzling hot into cold water. The sudden queer shapes which the hot lead assumes as it is poured into the cold water is supposed to contain the solution to her problem. Wearing the bone of the bat assures luck in love. The sweet-smelling crackling of cloves on live embers will help rid a victim of evil spirits.

Amulets are worn all over Greece to ward off the evil eye. Animals used as beasts of burden are also adorned with these amulets. They are generally blue beads placed on the brow of the animal very decoratively, but plainly to be seen by all. The baby cap of every infant is adorned with blue beads, gold coins and garlic. When a person expresses admiration for another, especially for a child, the mother will say quickly "spit" or "garlic in your eyes!" Admiration is so likely to be a disguise for envy. The charm is worn by many as protection against demons.

The folk songs on magic and witchcraft hold a high place in the villager's repertory of songs, not only because they are delightfully entertaining, but because they are often used as a weapon by the older generation to restrain incredulous, realistic youngsters disdainful of these traditions and irreverent toward their sources. One of the most popular of these songs has come down to us from Byzantine times:

THE WITCH'S DAUGHTER

Dear black swallows and dear white birds,
dip down from where you are flying high.
I would give you a message to take to my home,
to give to my darling and to my mother,
not to expect me, not to wait for me.
For they have wedded me here, in this foreign land,
to a sorcerer's daughter, a witch's child.
She charms the ships and they do not sail,
she charms the rowboats and they do not move,
she charms me too and I cannot come.
When I prepare to leave,—snows and floods,
and when I return,—sun and starbeams.
I saddle my horse,—the saddle slips.
I gird on my weapons—they fall to the ground.

The village wedding is a gay, colorful and communal celebration. The bride's trousseau is carried through the streets by people hired for the occasion. If the bride comes from another village, the trousseau is carried on mules. Furniture, the bride's dowry (the old Greek word for this was paraphernalia), is piled high on open carriages as it is moved to the bride's new home. The trousseau is then displayed in the best room of the house and all the villagers drop in to wish the couple happiness and to admire especially those articles which have been embroidered or woven by the hands of the bride. After the ceremony, the newlyweds walk through the streets accompanied by fiddlers and swarms of villagers. At the feast, the foamy ritsina flows freely and the guests join in song and dance to bless the union. At such a time, you are likely to hear nuptial songs that remind one of the epithalamia of the ancients. The Wedding Song *included here has come down to us from Byzantine times:*

THE WEDDING SONG

The sun fell in love and married the moon,
and he invited his in-laws the stars to the feast,
fluffed out the clouds for them to sit,
served them a feast of nectar and flowers,
seas and rivers of wine to drink.
All the stars were there but the star of morning;
and at dawn the morning star appeared,
bearing a gift of lively sleep for the bride and groom
and lanterns to light the in-laws on their way,
to leave and return to their homes; the newlyweds are sleepy.

The Greeks have always been passionately patriotic. And each time they have succeeded in ridding their sun-flooded land of covetous invaders, they have commemorated in song the heroes who fought against the enemy. Angelos Sikelianos once told a group of army men at Komotini, in Thrace, that the battles of Salamis and Thermopylae stand out with peculiar radiance because the soldiers were themselves Delphic Initiates, fighting not only for the physical boundaries of

Greece but for the Hellenic idea of one world. Greeks have always been conscious of the ultimate necessity of one world. Perhaps this explains, too, why the Greek people succeeded in ridding their nation of the superior mechanized army of the Italians in the Albanian campaign of 1941 with only a small infantry force of barefooted, ragged and starving soldiers who gained new strength from their war-cry "aera" as they tossed their enemies over the cliffs of the Pindos. Patriotism is the mighty stream that nourishes the creative life of the Greeks.

Digenis Akritas was the hero who guarded the frontiers of Byzantinum against invaders. The valiant exploits of this hero made him so renowned that in the literature of the demotike he epitomizes the bravery of all the ancient heroes. The Digenis Akritas epic consists of about 5000 lines and was written in the eleventh century though the author is not definitely known. The action takes place in the Byzantine Empire: Syria, Cappadocia and the Euphrates. The poem gives a picture of the political, social and military life of the Byzantine Greeks in the 10th century and glorifies the splendor of Byzantine life under the Macedonian Dynasty (867-1081). Besides the Digenis Akritas epic, there is the Akritic cycle made up of several hundred poems which recount the glorious exploits of the companions of Digenis.

Digenis (meaning double-birth), was the son of a Christian noblewoman and a Syrian Emir. Legend has it that Digenis was destined never to be conquered by any mortal man. One night while he was guarding a frontier, Death accosted him and commanded him to prepare to part with his soul. Digenis refused to do so before they had fought it out on a marble threshing floor. They agreed that only if Death conquered Digenis would his soul be taken. The fight lasted three whole days and three nights. At the end of these three days and nights, Digenis conquered Death. The Akritan hero then raised his hands to thank God for his victory. At that moment

Death, transformed into a golden eagle, perched on the head of Digenis, caught him by the hair and dragged his soul down to the lower world. One of the most popular of the Digenis songs is on the death of the Akritan hero:

DIGENIS

Digenis lies dying and the earth is terrified.
The heaven thunders and flashes, the upper world quakes.
The nether world gapes, the foundations crumble,
the tombstone shudders—how will it cover him,
how will it cover the eagle, bravest of the earth?
No house could hold him, no cave could keep him.
He strode over mountains, he leaped over peaks,
played with mountain sides, tossed boulders,
caught the soaring bird, the falcon in flight,
antelopes and beasts, running and leaping.
Death, secretly jealous and treacherous, trailed him
to pierce his heart and snatch his soul.

The glory of Byzantine architecture was the great basilica of Saint Sophia in Constantinople, built by order of the Emperor Justinian (527-565). It is said that when the Turks entered the basilica in Constantinople on that fateful day of May 29, 1453, the last mass was being celebrated. At the sight of the enemy soldiers, the priest walked up to the gallery of the Catechumen carrying the chalice in his hands. A door opened. He entered and immediately disappeared. Legend has it that he is still waiting for the day when the basilica of Saint Sophia will be restored to its original faith. It is said, too, that at the last moment of the interrupted mass, tears poured from the icon of the Holy Virgin. The incident is recorded in the following song:

THE FALL OF CONSTANTINOPLE

God proclaims a paean, earth and the heavens resound,
and Saint Sophia, the great basilica, rings out
with four hundred carillons and sixty-two bells,
each bell has a priest, each priest has a deacon,
to intone the Cherubic Hymn for the King to come forth.
Doves fly down from the highest heaven:
"Cease the Cherubic Hymn, let the holy vessel be lowered,
for God wills that Constantinople fall to the Turks.
Only send word to the west for three ships to come,
one to carry the Cross, another the Gospel,
the third, the best, our Holy Altar,
lest the dogs loot and desecrate it."

The Virgin grieves and the icons weep.
"Hush, Holy Mother of God, and you, icons, cease your
[weeping,
Again, with the years, in time, again they will be Thine!"

The songs written in the vernacular during the four centuries of Turkish domination (1453-1821) were chiefly ballads of the klephts who lived on the mountains of Olympos, Pindos, Pelion, and other areas. These ballads were created either by the klephts themselves or by rhapsodists who were present during the events that these songs celebrate. They sang them at village feasts very much as did the rhapsodists of ancient Greece. The klephtic ballads are highly poetic and imaginative and reveal the rugged and precarious life of the klephts who fought to free Greece. They reveal too, the bitter hatred felt for the Turks, the love they bore their comrades, their home and nation. Two of the most popular of these klephtic songs are the Death of the Klep

THE DEATH OF THE KLEPHT

Eat and drink, my comrades, rejoice and let us be gay,
nothing ails me but a wound!
How bitter is the wound, how venomous the bullet!
Come, lift me up and set me yonder.
Come, some of you brave lads, and take me
and carry me up to a high hill.
Strew green branches; then set me down,
and from the priests fetch me sweet wine
to wash the wound, for I am hurt,
and take my knife, my silver scimitar,
and dig my grave and build my coffin,
wide, long, roomy enough for two
to stand erect, fight, take cover, reload,
and on my right side, leave a window,
so that birds may fly in and out, the nightingales of Spring.

Kitsos, one of the most loved folk songs, shows the hero, with his mother, when he is about to be put to death. It reveals the courage of the klephts, male and female alike, who while stoically facing death, seek to preserve the means by which new hands may fight the enemy. In this poem, the mother shows more concern over the loss of her son's weapons than over his untimely death.

KITSOS

Kitsos's mother sits at the river's edge,
quarreling with the river and stoning it:
"River please, lower your tide, river flow back,
let me cross over to the klephtic villages,
where the klephts are meeting in their fastnesses."

THE FOLK SONG: SOURCE OF MODERN GREEK POETRY 53

Kitsos is taken; the enemy will hang him.
A thousand walk before him and two thousand behind.
And far in the rear walks his sorrowing little mother,
lamenting and imploring, lamenting and imploring:

"Kitsos, my son, where are your arms, your poor equipment?"
"Foolish mother, mad mother, witless mother,
you should weep for my lost youth, for my wasted manhood,
but you weep only for my poor arms, my poor equipment."

For the Greek people, death is darkness. There is no song about heaven among the demotic songs. None of the metaphysics of Christianity enters into their poetry. In their folk songs on death, the Greeks sing for a better world in this life. Indeed, the most heroic struggle of the Greeks has been against Death itself. In their folk songs they talk with Death, address him with respect but never with servility. Invariably, Death outsmarts his victim by treachery. One of the popular demotic songs about death tells of a man who houses his beloved in a stone fortress and goes out himself to meet Death and plead with him for her:

Arise, beloved, let us go, beloved, let us go
to a high mountain, high up on a mountain top,
to build a marble fort that will shut you in,
and if Death should come and find you, I will face him.
I will go out, hold his horse's reins and kiss his hand;
"Kind Death, can one bribe or entreat you,
can mothers run to you with gold coins or sisters with pennies,
or wives of brave men with priceless jewels?"

"What talk is this, my little man, what talk is this?
Am I a town official, a tax-collector?
They call me Death, they call me Home Destroyer.

Where there are three I take two, where there are two, I
[take one,
and where there is but one, I pull the door to and close it,
and strangers take the keys, strangers inherit."

In keeping with the attitude of the Greek people towards death is their idea of the supernatural. In The Vampire, *Constantine, who returns from the grave, has lost his hair, his manly moustache. He is horrible to look at and frightens not only his sister, but the birds of the air who comment on the world of the living and the dead. A vampire, in ancient belief, was the reincarnation of a dead person unable to rest until a vow or social obligation had been fulfilled. In this poem, the son is exhorted to rise from the dead to fulfill a pledge to the mother. The son fulfills his awful duty, but Death takes his toll for the temporary abrogation of his powers. The exquisite music of the poem, its deep melancholy, make it one of the favorite folk songs. It is sung especially in the Dodecanese and was written in the post-Byzantine period:*

THE VAMPIRE

Mother with your nine sons and your only daughter,
your daughter dear, and only, and much beloved,
twelve years you had her and the sun never saw her;
you washed her in the shadow, you combed her in the dark,
by evening star and morning star you curled her hair.
When from Babylon they brought you marriage offers
to marry her afar, in very distant foreign lands . . .
Eight brothers were against it, but Constantine agreed:
"Give her in marriage, Mother, let Arete go to foreign lands.
Then when to foreign lands I travel, to foreign lands I go,
I will find refuge, a little house to stay."
"Constantine you are wise, but now your words are foolish,

for if death, my son, should visit me, or wasting disease,
sorrow or joy should come, who will bring her home?"
God he made his guarantor, the saints his witnesses,
if death or illness should befall,
come weal or woe, he'd bring her home.

And when in a foreign land Arete was wedded
a lean year came and angry months,
and plague followed and the nine brothers died.
The mother found herself alone, a single stalk in the field.
Over the eight graves she beat her breast, she mourned,
at the grave of Constantine she lifted the tombstone:
"Constantine arise! I must have my Arete! . . .
God you made your guarantor, the saints your witnesses,
come weal or woe, you would bring her home."
Her prayer raised him from the coffin!
He made the clouds his horse, the stars his baldric,
the moon his companion, and he went to bring her.
He left the mountains behind, yet peaks rose before him,
under the crescent moon, he found her combing her hair.
He greeted her from afar and from afar addressed her:
"Come, my little Arete, for our mother needs you."
"Woe is me, brother dear, why at this hour!
If it is for joy, I shall wear my gold,
and if it is for sorrow, tell me, and I will come as I am."
"Come, my little Arete, come as you are." . . .
On the road they traveled, the road they walked,
they heard birds singing, they heard birds saying:
"How strange to see a dead man lead a fair live maid!"
"Hearken, my Constantine, to what the birds are saying:
'How strange to see a dead man lead a fair live maid!'"
"They are witless birds, let them chatter,
they are foolish birds, let them talk."
And as they went farther, other birds took up the cry:

"What do we birds see to our sorrow!
The living walking hand in hand with the dead!"
"Do you hear, my Constantine, what the birds are saying?
'How the living are walking hand in hand with the dead!'"
"They are fledglings, let them chatter,
they are fledglings, let them prate."
O brother dear, you frighten me, your breath is incense-laden!"
"Last night when we went to the Church of St. John,
the priest sprinkled incense with liberal hands . . ."
And as they went farther, other birds took up the cry:
"Almighty God, what wonders you endlessly perform,
to let a dead man lead such a fair and graceful girl!"
Once more Arete heard it and her spirits sank:
"Do you hear, my Constantine, what the birds are saying?
Tell me, where is your hair, your manly moustache?"
"I suffered from a fever, that brought me close to death,
my blonde hair fell out and my manly moustache."

They found the house locked, securely bolted,
and the windows of the house thick with cobwebs:
"Unbar the door, dear Mother, your Arete is here!"
"Go if you are Death, I have no sons for you,
and Arete dwells afar in a land of strangers.
"Unbar the door, dear mother, it is I, your Constantine.
God I made my guarantor, the saints my witnesses,
come weal or woe, I'd lead her back to you!" . . .
Before she could unbar the door, Death had stepped inside.

EROTOKRITOS

excerpt

EROTOKRITOS:

Excerpt from the 17th Century Masterpiece in the Vernacular

Erotokritos *the epic poem of 11,000 lines composed by Vincenzo Kornaros in 1650 is considered the most important of the literary masterpieces of the Cretan cycle of the 17th century. It is regarded by all Greeks as an integral part of their historic and linguistic struggle and is so popular with the Greek people that many know whole sections of it by heart. The poet, Kostes Palamas called* Erotokritos *the "great epic of the modern Greek people." Set in ancient Athens, it tells of the love of Aretousa (or Arete as she was popularly called), daughter of King Heracles of Athens, and Erotokritos, son of Pezostratos, a poor man who had been raised to the position of councillor to the king. The story is a romantic portrayal of life in the post-Byzantine era. In spite of the many valiant exploits of Erotokritos the King of Athens considered him undesirable as a husband for his daughter and issued on order to banish him from the kingdom. The passage selected here shows Erotokritos on the night before he must leave. He meets Aretousa at their accustomed haunt, tells her of his banishment and his love for her:*

BOOK III—Lines 1337-1406

Aretousa much desires that the day turn to night,
that the night find her, that they plan for the wedding.
Erotokritos too is burning with desire
to speak with her of his banishment,
for he is still unsure of Arete's heart,
he is seized with fear, alarm, disquiet.
He thinks when he is exiled, and gone far away,
Arete will quench the blaze of their love.
So each man who loves must live in fear
for often desire has been forgot,
and he who loves truly, it matters not who,
ever is fearful his love will betray him.
The evening came, and then the night, they pined
to be at the window, to share their woes.
Midnight arrived, the appointed hour,
they hied to the spot where each night they met.
First for an hour they wept much, they sobbed,
and then amidst their sighs, they recounted their sorrows.
Erotokritos spoke: "Have you heard the sad news?
Your father has exiled me, I must walk foreign roads.
When he heard the marriage offer my father made for me,
he wished he were dead, so grieved was he
so harsh a blow it seemed to him,
I feel my own father in sorrow will die for this!
Only four days of grace have been granted me,
then I must depart, flee this land.
How can I go from you, leave you behind,
how can I live in that exile without you?
You will hear, my beloved, that my end has come,
in a foreign land they bury me, there my bones lie.
I know your father will soon want you to wed,
 e seeks a prince, your peer in wealth and title,

EROTOKRITOS

and you cannot resist, when your parents command,
they bend your will, and your desire changes,
my lady, one boon I ask, one thing alone I crave,
grant me this boon, and I'll gladly meet death.
When your parents betroth you, sigh for me,
and when in bridal dress they array you,
and once wedded, you change your attire,
let the tears fall and say: 'Poor Erotokritos,
my vows to you are forgotten, your wish cannot be!'
And when you give yourself to this groom
and he becomes lord of your beauty
and kisses, embraces you with passion,
remember the one who died for you,
remember that you wounded me
and that I suffered the pangs of death
though I never touched you with the shadow of my hand.
And once a month, within your room,
give thought to what I suffered, let your heart feel for me,
take up the painting that is in your drawer,
and the songs I sang that you admired,
and read and look and think of me,
whom they sent to dwell afar because of you,
and when you hear I am no more, weep and mourn,
and burn in the fire the songs I wrote,
for then no longer will there be a cause
to cherish them, then let them be forgot.
I beseech you to heed well what I say to you now,
I am leaving you soon, I am leaving this land.
Let me, unfortunate, pretend I never saw you,
but held a candle lit and now snuffed out.
But as long as life endures, wherever fate may lead,
I swear never to gaze on another, nor lift my eyes to her,
death for your sake is sweeter than life with another.
My body was born on earth for you alone.

So has your beauty stirred within my eyes,
so has love painted you within them,
that wherever I stand, wherever my eyes turn,
I can see nought but your image before me.
This you must believe—when I am dying,
should I hear you call, then will I live again."

Modern Greek Poetry

RHIGAS PHERAIOS

1751-1798. Also named Rhigas Velestinli. Born in Velestino. Called the "Tyrtaeos of Modern Greece." Studied in Thessaly and became head of the village school of Kissos. He published School of Delicate Lovers *(1790)* Anthology of Physics *(1791). Rhigas drew up an insurrectionary proclamation basing the future constitution of Greece upon the French Revolution. He went to Moldavia, Wallachia, to rally the people around the idea of Balkan Unity which would include the Turks on a democratic basis. Later, he was seized by the Austrians, turned over to the Turks and strangled to death at Belgrade in 1798.*

WAR HYMN

How long, my heroes, shall we live in bondage,
alone like lions on ridges, on peaks?
Living in caves, seeing our children
turned from the world to bitter enslavement?
Losing our land, brothers, and parents,
our friends, our children and all our relations?
Better an hour of life that is free
than forty years in slavery!
What does it profit you to live enslaved?
Think how they sear you each hour in the fire—
official, dragoman, even a vizier—
the tyrant unjustly tries to destroy you.
Let Soutsos, Mourizis, Petrakis, Skanavis,
Gikas, Mavroyanis be mirrors for you to see.

Come now with zest,
take the oath on the cross.

We must choose able advisors
to build a government for the people.
Our first and only guide must be Law,
the only leader of our nation.
For anarchy, too, resembles bondage;
living like wild beasts is a fiercer torment.
Then with hands raised to the sky,
let us swear this oath to God from our hearts.
"O King of the world, I swear to Thee,
never to heed the tyrant's words,
neither to work for him, nor to be by him beguiled,
never to yield to his promises.
And if I am forsworn, may lightning strike
and burn me till I vanish like smoke.
As long as I am on earth, my sole purpose
to annihilate them will be unshaken.
Loyal to my land, I will break the chains,
standing at my leader's side.
And if I am forsworn, may lightning strike
and burn me till I vanish like smoke.

In the east, west, south and north,
let all have one heart for one land.
Let each worship God in the fashion he pleases,
let us hasten together to the glory of war,
let each whom tyranny has exiled
now return to his own.
Bulgarians, Albanians, Armenians, Greeks,
black and white, let us belt the sword
all together in a surge for freedom,
so the world will know that we are the brave!
How did our forefathers surge like lions,
leaping for liberty into the fire?
So we, brothers too, must seize our arms

and cast off at once this bitter slavery,
to slay the wolves who impose the yoke,
and cruelly torture Christian and Turk.
Let the Cross shine on land and sea,
let justice make the enemy kneel,
let the world be healed of this grievous wound,
and let us live on earth as brothers—free.

YIANNIS VILARAS

1771-1823. Born in Yanina, Epirus. He specialized in medicine and studied Italian literature at Padua. He was physician to Veli Pasha, son of Ali Pasha, famous governor of Yanina. A staunch demoticist, he wrote a book entitled The Greek Vernacular *(1814). He wrote* Characters *and made adaptations from Aesop's Fables. Vilaras's fame as a writer rests chiefly on the fact that he had the courage to break with the purist and participate militantly in the struggle to make the spoken tongue the official language of Greece. The sack of Yanina by Kourshid Pasha in 1822 robbed him of his property and he died in extreme poverty.*

SPRING

Sweetest spring
adorned in flowers,
wreathed in roses,
gazes gently on the earth.

As the green clothes the earth,
the forests become shadier,
the cold snows melt,
the sky laughs.

The little flowers wear their colors,
the slopes are colored too,
the cool-breathed dawns
shed voluptuous light.

On the thorny rose
the nightingale dulcetly sings,
the foreign swallow
builds his nest.

In the fields and green meadows
the lively flocks,
many and tireless,
bleat and leap.

The blithe young shepherd
playing the flute
fills the breeze
with the voice of song.

Each soul rejoices,
honors the spring.
Thyrsis is sullen
in the general joy.

Pretty Daphne, arise
as a final adornment;
then Thyrsis will be
happiest of all.

ANDREAS CALVOS

1792-1867. Born in Zante. Went to Italy when very young where he received a scientific education. His first poems were written in Italian. He wrote two Italian tragedies. He returned to Corfu in 1826 where he became first a director of a school, then professor of philosophy at the Ionian University. Two years after the Greek Revolution broke out, Calvos published The Lyre, *his first collection of odes in Greek, inspired by the patriotic fervour of the times.* New Odes *appeared in 1826. Calvos wrote sometimes in the neo-purist Greek idiom and sometimes in the demotic. Most of his poems are patriotic. His mission was to immortalize the heroes who fell for Greece. He died in England.*

THE LOVER OF HIS COUNTRY

O dearly loved land,
O marvelous island,
Zante! You who granted me
the breath of Apollo
and his golden gifts!

Hear now my song;
for immortals abhor
ungrateful men
and hurl thunderbolts
on their heads.

Never did I forget you,
though fate cast me
far from you—a fifth
of a century found me
in foreign lands.

But good fortune or bad,
when the lilies adorned
the mountains and waves,
you were always
before my eyes.

When night covers
the rose of heaven
with the blackest cloak
you are the only joy
of my dreams.

O blessed Ausonian land
where the sun once
brightened my steps
and the clear breeze
always smiled!

There the people were happy.
The maidens of Parnassos
danced and the leaves
of their lilies
crowned the lyre.

On the rocks of Albion,
the wild swollen waters
of the ocean roll
and run and break and dash
impetuously.

The horn of Amalthaea
pours power and glory
and measureless wealth
on the banks of the
renowned Thames.

The Aeolian breeze
carried me there.
By rays of sweetest
Liberty was I reared
and attended.

I admired your temples, too,
holy city of the Celts.
You lack no
Aphrodite of the mind,
of the spirit.

Hail Ausonia, and to you
Albion hail; to you
glorious Paris, hail!
But Zante, beautiful and unique,
possesses me.

The forests of Zante
and her shadowy mountains
once heard the twang
of Diana's divine
silver arrows.

And even today the shepherds
venerate the trees
and the fresh springs,
for sea-nymphs still
wander there.

Here the Ionian wave first
kissed Aphrodite's body,
the Ionian breezes
first caressed
her breast.

And when the evening star
lights the sky
and sea-going vessels
float full of love
and voices raise in song,

the same kisses,
and the same breezes caress
the body and the breast
of the flower of loveliness—
the Virgins of Zante.

Your vine smells sweet,
oh my beloved land,
and the ocean is enriched
by the fragrance
of golden citron trees.

The king of immortals
has granted you
grape-bearing roots
and clouds diaphanous
light and clear.

In the daytime the eternal torch
nurtures your fruit,
and the tears
of night become
lilies on you.

If sometimes on your features
the snow falls, it melts soon.
The torrid Dog Star
never withers
your emeralds.

You are blessed and more,
I call you most blessed,
for you never knew
the hard lash of the foe,
or the tyrant.

Let not fate grant me
a grave on a foreign soil;
death is sweet
only when a man sleeps
in his own land.

TO THE SACRED BATTALION

(300 students formed The Sacred Battalion, *one month before the Greek War of Independence of 1821, and went to Bucharest to assist Alexander Ypsilante, a Russian General of Greek birth. The Turks cut them down almost to a man.)*

May rain clouds never burst;
may the harsh wind
never disperse
the blessed earth
covering you.

May the rose-veiled goddess
refresh it always
with her silver tears.
Here may the flowers
sprout forever.

O true sons of Greece,
souls that valiantly
fell in combat,

picked company of heroes,
pride of all youth!

Fate snatched from you
the victor's laurel,
wove for you instead
a crown of myrtle
and funeral cypress.

But when men die
for their country
the cypress boughs are fair
and the myrtle leaf
is priceless,

ever since provident nature
poured fear
and golden hope
and the day
into the eyes of the first man.

On the vast face
of the verdant earth
the eyes of heaven
soon saw thousands
of deeply dug graves.

Most things are hidden;
the star of immortality
shines over only a few;
the gods alone can give man
freedom to choose.

Greeks, worthy of your land
and your ancestors,
you Greeks, how could
an inglorious grave be
chosen for you?

The envious old man Time,
the foe of all works
and each shrine,
comes and girds the sea
and the earth.

Out of the urn he pours
the currents of Lethe
and all is wiped out.
Cities crumble, realms
and nations are lost.

But when he approaches
the earth that holds you
Time will take another road,
in reverence
of your honored earth.

Here shall mothers
bring their children
when we restore to Greece
her ancient purple
and her sceptre.

And weeping they shall
kiss the sacred dust
and say, "Strive my sons
to equal the glorious Battalion,
the Battalion of Heroes."

THE OCEAN

Earth of Greece, child of the Gods,
mother of heroes,

dear, sweet land,
a night of slavery enfolded you,
a night of centuries.

So over the boundless chaos
of the sky's desolate regions,
black Erebus
spread wide
mourning veils.

And in the deep darkness,
in the infinite space,
the soft lights
of the stars
moved in sorrow.

Cities perished,
forests were lost,
and the sea slept
and the mountains; and the bustle
of the living ceased.

In the realms of darkness
all creation
resembles death; from there
no sound ever comes,
neither songs nor dirges.

But see! The Hours throw open
the balustrade of dawn.
See! The tireless horses
of the sun come out
of the blessed stables.

Golden, flaming
challenging hoofs
burn the roads of the wind.

The skies are lit
by shining manes.

Now the dawn opens
the flowers in the dewy
breast of the earth;
and now appear the works
of industrious men.

The fragrant lips
of day kiss
earth's restful brow.
Dreams and darkness
depart.

Sleep and silence; then once more
the fields, the ocean,
the wind and the towns
and the cities are filled with noise,
flocks and lyres.

See, at the mouth of the cave
the great Lion
appears roaring.
It shakes its frightful
shaggy head.

The eagle soars from
the high cliffs;
its wings beat the clouds,
and their threshing
shatters Olympos.

A night of many centuries
desolated Greece,
a night of long slavery,
through infamy of men or will
of the Immortals.

The land appeared then
like a temple in ruins
where psalms are silenced
and the ivy leaves
untrembling, sleep.

As if on the endless sea,
the sea of dreams,
a few desperate
souls of the dead passed
leisurely.

Thus, three-faced Hecate
slowly rolling the chariot
across the sky
from the trees
of Mount Athos

to the rocks of Cytherea,
beheld the ships
yielding ingloriously,
leaving dispersed,
the Aegean gulfs.

Then you, most sparkling daughter
of Zeus, sole consolation
of the world,
you remembered my land,
O Liberty.

The goddess came; down she came
to the enclosed shores
of Chios; she stretched forth
her arms and weeping,
she said:

"Ocean, father of
immortal dances,
hear my voice,
and grant me the great
desire of my soul.

"My glorious throne
in Greece tyrants
have held for generations.
Help me today!
Restore my throne.

"When I have fled
foolish mortals, your fatherly
embrace receives me;
On your love rests
all my hope."

She spoke, and then
she sped over the ocean
tides, lighting
its waters, its god-like back
in a vivid gleam.

The waves sparkled
as the heavens, and the sun
shone cloudless and starry
revealing the many islands
of the Aegean.

Behold now! The war-cry
rises like a strong
wind in the forests;
Hear the rising cheers
of the sailors.

Furrowed by thousands of prows
the sea foams,
the winged spindles
spread freely
in the breeze.

Thus at dawn
swarms of bees fly
on the lake
when the sweet spring
breezes blow.

Thus the lions pace
on the sand
seeking out the flocks,
once they feel the heat
of their claws.

Thus when the eagles hear
the strength of their wings,
proudly they scorn
the thundering
roar.

Beloved offspring
of the ocean; brave
and true sons of Greece
and leaders
of liberty,

hail, you pride
of the wonderful reefs
(Spetsai, Hydra, Psara)
where fear of peril
never docked.

Good fortune! Send forth
the swift ships
of valiant men;
scatter, burn
the barbarian fleet.

Scorn the cowardly hordes
of your enemies!
Triumph always crowns
the brow of those who risk danger
for their native land.

O heavenly land!
I see you—a steersman
at the dread helm.
See how the prows
of heroes fly!

See, they break, they smash
the floating castles
of countless foes;
the flame devours hulls,
sailors, masts, sails.

And the sea swallows
the corpses. Oh lyre,
exalt the victory. When heroes
win glory, the gods
love paeans.

O haughty Turks
where are you now? Assemble and dispatch
a new fleet, fools!
The Greeks will seize
a new laurel!

DIONYSIOS SOLOMOS

1798-1857. Born in Zante. He is named by many "The Dante of Greece" and by Goethe "The Byron of the East." He is unquestionably the national poet of Modern Greece. All of Solomos's writings are in defense of the free spirit of man. The son of a wealthy nobleman, he was educated at the University of Padua and wrote his first verses in Italian. With the uprising of the people against the Turks, he turned his attention to the vernacular and fought to make this the official language of Greece. His first poem written in the vernacular was Xanthoula. *In 1824, three years after the Greek Revolution broke out, Solomos wrote* The Hymn to Liberty *which consists of 158 verses. The Hymn is now the national anthem of Greece and has been translated into Italian, French and English. When Byron died, Solomos wrote a long hymn* On the Death of Lord Byron. The Free Besieged *is considered the greatest achievement of his life and occupied him at least 20 years.* The Dialogue *is an impassioned prose conversation between a poet and a pedant, in defense of the demotic language.* The Destruction of Psara *was written in 1824 after the total massacre of that island by the Turks. Other Works:* Ode to Marco Botsaris *(fragment),* Lambros *(fragments),* The Cretan *(fragments),* The Woman of Zante *was not discovered until 1927.* The Girl in Solitude *(1829),* Poisoned Girl *(1826),* The Dream, *a satiric poem,* To Francesca Frazer. Complete Works *have been edited by Jacob Polylas. G. Kalosgourou edited and translated* Italian Poems. *Kostas Varnalis published a critical work about Dionysios Solomos entitled* Solomos Without Metaphysics. *Kostes Palamas edited Solomos's works in 1901.*

THE DESTRUCTION OF PSARA

(written in 1824, after the total massacre of this island by the Turks.)

> On the charred earth of Psara,
> Glory roams alone,
> musing on her warrior-heroes,
> wearing a wreath on her hair
> made of a few dry weeds
> left on the desolate earth.

I WALKED THE ROAD OF THE DAWN
(from THE FREE BESIEGED)

I walked the road of the dawn,
the road of the Sun,
the lyre of justice
thrown over my shoulder,
all the way from sunrise
to sundown.

TEMPTATION (from THE FREE BESIEGED)

Love dances with yellow-haired April;
it is nature's good, sweet season,
and in the swelling shadows enfolding dew and musk
are languorous bird songs yet unheard.
Clear, sweet, graceful waters
pour into the musk-scented abyss,
taking its musk and leaving its freshness,

all revealing the wealth of their source to the sun,
darting here, there, like nightingales.
So too life gushes forth on earth, and sky and wave.
But on the waters of the lake, white and still,
still as far as the eye can see and clear to the depths,
the butterfly which makes its fragrant bed within the heart
of the wild lily, sports with its small strange shadow.
"Lovely dreamer, tell me what you have seen this night?"
"A night full of wonder, a night sown with magic!
No movement on earth or skies or seas,
not even as much as the bee makes near the tiny flower.
Around something motionless, whitening in the lake,
only the full moon moved
and a graceful girl rises clothed in its light."

TO FRANCESCA FRAZER

A humble poet looked upon a maiden,
and spoke to his inmost happy self;
"Fair maiden, though the stones grow lilies for your feet,
the sun braid a golden wreath for your head,
they have no fitting gift for you and your inner wealth,
Oh world of beauty, chaste, wrought by the angels!"

HYMN TO LIBERTY

(Written in 1823, it consists of 158 stanzas, the first 16 of which are translated here. In these stanzas, Liberty is described rising from the bones of all Greek heroes who have died in her defense.)

I know you by the blade
of your dread sword,
I know you by your eye
swiftly surveying the world.

Risen from the bones,
a hallowed Greek trail,
and valiant as of old,
Hail, O Liberty, hail!

Down there you lived,
shy, in bitter pain,
waiting for some voice,
to tell you, 'Rise again!'

That day was long delayed;
shrouded with a pall,
for fear had terrorized
and slavery weighed over all.

Wretched! Your only consolation
allowed you to keep,
to recount your past glory,
and narrating it to weep.

And waiting, ever waiting,
for that voice of the free,
wringing hand in hand,
waiting hopelessly.

You said: "When shall I lift
my head out of this desolation?"
The answer came from overhead,
shrieks, chains, lamentation.

Then you raised your eyes
dimmed by your tears

saw your dress wet with blood,
Greek blood, wet with the years.

I know in secret you started
for foreign lands,
in your dress blood-drenched
seeking help from other hands.

Alone you trudged the road,
you returned alone.
When rattled by need,
doors are unyielding as stone.

Another wailed at your breast,
none offered to relieve you;
another promised you help,
and frightfully deceived you.

Alas, in your adversity
others maliciously jeered.
"Go on, go find your sons,
Go," the hard-hearted sneered.

Back turned your footsteps,
rapidly falling,
every blade, every stone,
your glory recalling.

Most humbled by sorrow
you bent your head low,
like the door-driven poor,
whose life is a woe.

Yes, but now each Greek son
fights with unshaken strength,
tirelessly seeking,
victory or death.

Risen from the bones,
a hallowed Greek trail,
and valiant as of old,
Hail O Liberty, hail!

THE CRETAN

(A Cretan tries to save his bride in a storm at sea. All the other members of his family have been killed by the Turks.)

. . . .
. . . .

I looked and the shore was still faraway.
Good lightning, flash once more!
Three lightning bolts fell, one after the other
very close to the maid with a deafening thunder;
sky and sea resounded with the thunder,
the shore and the mountains with all their voices.
Believe what I say is gospel truth,
by the many wounds that devoured my breast,
by the comrades who fell warring in Crete,
by the soul that destroyed me when it left the world.
(Blow, bugle! while I shake out the shroud,
and I tear down the road to call to the rising mists:
"Have you seen the beauty who blesses the Valley?
Tell me and may you be blessed with all you deserve.
There is no mist left on earth; a new sky is born;
I love her as of old, and I will stand beside her at the Judg-
[ment Seat."
"We saw her on high in the morning; the flowers fluttered
at the gate of Paradise whence she came forth with songs
chanting the Resurrection joyously;
her spirit eager to re-enter her body.

The whole firmament listened dazzled,
the world in flames restrained its burning.
And now she appeared before us; moving swiftly,
but she looked now here, now there as if seeking someone.")

It still thundered . . .
But the sea that heaved like seething water,
calmed, became entirely still and clear,
fragrant as a garden, mirroring the stars.
Some secret force constrained nature
to adorn herself with beauty and put aside her rage.
No breath stirred in the sky, the sea,
not even as much as the passing bee sucking a flower.
But near the maiden joyfully clasping me close,
the full clear moon shuddered;
and from it something quickly unwinds
and before me appears a moon-dressed maiden.
The fresh light flickered on her god-like features,
on her live black eyes and golden hair.

She looked at the stars and they were filled with joy;
they cast their rays on her yet left her uncovered;
lightly she lifted her cypress like body;
from the sea she stepped without stirring a ripple.
And she opened her arms with love and modesty
revealing all her beauty, her graciousness.
Then night was flooded as with the light of noon;
all creation became a temple everywhere gleaming.
At last she turned to me standing before her
in midstream as the compass facing the North,
Not toward the maid, but toward me she bent her head;
unlucky me, I gazed at her; she gazed at me,
I thought I had seen her far in the past,
painted in some temple in awe-struck wonder
or wrought by my mind most lovingly

or dreamed in a dream at my mother's breast.
She was an old sweet, forgotten memory,
but now she comes towards me in all her strength
like the sun-adorned water the eye sees dashing
fiercely against the mountain's base.
My tear-filled eyes were blurred,
and for a long time I was blind to that divine face,
but I felt her glance piercing my quivering heart
and silencing me.
But such is the power of gods and from their high abodes
they can probe the abyss as well as man's heart,
and I felt she read my mind better
than if I were to tell her with my bitter lips:
"Look deep within my soul where sorrow blooms."

. . . .
. . . .

"But my heart is flooded to the depths;
the Turks seized my stalwart brothers,
dishonored my sister then straightway slew her,
burnt my aged father at night,
and at dawn flung my mother into the well,
in Crete. . . .
I filled my hands with its earth and went far from there.
Help me goddess, only to hold the frail branch;
I hang from a steep cliff and cling only to that."

Sweetly she smiled at my heart's pain,
tears clouded the eyes which resembled my loved one's.
She is lost, woe is me! but I felt her tear fall
on the hand I lifted as soon as I saw her.
From that moment I no longer have the hand
that sought a knife when the Turk approached;
war is no joy to it; I stretch it asking for bread
from the passerby who comes toward me in tears;

and when crushed by misfortune, my eyes dim slowly
and harsh dreams bring her back to life,
and the lightning strikes on the raging sea
and the sea tries to swallow the maiden,
I awake in a frenzy, sit up, my mind almost leaves me,
I extend my hand and at once the sea calms;
I tear through the wild, briny waves
with strength my youth never had in its prime,
not even when we fought in battle drawing swords,
a few brave lads in close combat with many,
nor when I struck at Bobo Yusuf and the two others
as I stepped recklessly close to the Labyrinth.
In the strain of the swimming, the beat of my heart,
and this increased it—pounded beside my beloved.

. . . .

. . . .

But I swim more feebly, numbed
by the sound, sweetest sound accompanying me.
It was no maiden's voice in a dense forest,
when the evening star appears and the waters cloud,
singing to nature her secret love
to the trees and the flowers that open and sway.
It was not a Cretan nightingale that raised its voice
to high and wild crags, where it builds its nest,
and through the night makes the distant sea and plain
thrill to the sweetness of his song
till the dawn appears and the stars melt
and she too hears and the roses fall from her hands.
It was not the sweet flute I heard when alone
on Mount Psiloriti where pain often drew me,
where I saw the heavenly star shine in mid-sky
and mountains smiling at it, the seas and valleys.
The hope of Liberty stirred deep within me,
and I cried: "O divine land, drenched with blood!"

And weeping, I stretched my hands to her in pride;
even her charred stone and dry grasses are fair.
No music, no bird, no voice can compare,
perhaps no sound like this exists on earth.
It was not the words nor the subtle sound . . .
The near-by echo could not send it back.
I could not tell if it came from near or far;
it filled the breeze like the fragrance of May,
sweet, ineffable . . .
Love and Death are not more potent.
So wholly it possessed my soul,
not sky, nor sea, nor shore nor girl
could enter.
It held me fast and often did I try
to rid me of my flesh to follow it.
At last it ceased, and nature felt the void.
And my soul, sighing, soon filled itself again with my beloved;
I carried my bride to the shore,
put her down with joy—she was dead.

THE DREAM (excerpt)

When the hands that scattered
the stars, created
the souls of mortals,
(and they created them well),
before all other feelings,
they gave them Compassion;
and you drove her out
to let Cruelty take her place
as you did the wretched widow
in your early years.

She advised you to take
the bread from the poor,
and to charge interest
many times over.
And the poor man, the outcast,
came to you in dread,
to tell you with his sorrowful
lips, "I have already paid it."
And he cast himself at your feet,
weeping countless tears, exposing
his wretched old age,
his wife, his children,
and their tattered clothes;
and you threw St. John's bread at him!
And thus, since you committed such crimes,
for forty-five years,
it is no wonder at all,
nor is the thing strange,
that you could hoard,
in the planks of your walls,
a mass of gold,
to rid you of fears.
But the curse of poverty,
most wretched of terrors,
will press on your soul
like the tombstone on your body.

EASTER DAY (from LAMBROS)

The last bright star of dawn
betokened a sun most clear,
nowhere in the sky

a trace of cloud or mist;
and the slow moving wind
blew so gently on the face,
it seemed to say to the heart's depths:
"Life is sweet and death is darkness."

Christ is risen! Young, old and girls,
all—little, tall, make ready!
Enter the laurel-laden churches,
gather together in the joyful light,
open your arms in peaceful embraces,
before the Saints and kiss each other!
Kiss sweetly lip to lip;
foes and friends say: *Christ is Risen!*

Each tombstone is covered with laurel,
and beautiful babes in their mothers' arms
stare at the painted icons.
The sweet-voiced choir chants;
the silver sparkles, the gold gleams
in the light of the candles;
each face glows from the holy candle
Christians carry in their hands.

MARIA'S PRAYER (from LAMBROS)

(Lambros has seduced Maria, a girl of fifteen whom he promises to marry but never does. They live together and she bears him four children, three sons and a daughter. After fifteen years, Lambros is still indifferent to her pleas to marry her. Lambros goes off to battle against Ali Pasha. Unknown to him he seduces his own daughter whom he recognizes by the cross Maria has branded on her palm. When she realizes

Lambros is her father, she throws herself into the lake. Lambros lets her drown. He returns home on the Eve of an Easter Sunday and finds Maria at church. Suddenly the shades of his three dead sons appear before him and force on him the Easter kiss. Repentant, he offers to marry Maria, but now she has lost her mind. He throws himself into the lake and Maria follows him.)

Now Maria came out to fill
her faded self with freshness.
The night is sweet and the moon
does not come out to obscure a single star.
Thousands shine in all their grace,
some apart, some set in clusters.
They too hail the Resurrection, as they dip
into the mirror of the glassy sea.

"I draw my hair across my withered breast.
I fold my hands, O powers above,
tell Him who is risen today
to have mercy on wretched Maria.
This is the day of love. Hell is conquered.
The nether world burns, the elements burn,
the world's blazing conflagration
casts its spark toward Him.

"Heaven resounds with Hallelujahs
and leans like a lover over the earth.
Even a drop of water clinging to the glass
lives; Hallelujah it and I.
When they heard the Gate break asunder,
what rumbling was there in the nether world?
Within, the abyss rejoices and whitens
Satan whistles at the Savior."

Meanwhile Lambros is in the church
where no breath other than his is heard.
He flits from one thought to another;
his mind a dismal, self-destroying world.
Slowly he rises from the choir-stall,
and a sigh escapes from within his heart.
Only the strewn laurel, fragrant,
crackles where he walks.

And his face grows yellow as sulphur,
and softly he utters these words:
"The Saints are deaf, unmoved like tombs.
I have spoken and cried until midnight.
Man (let fate decree what it will)
is his own God. This he reveals
at the brink of misfortune. Despair,
stay hidden and sleep in my soul."

Slowly he starts for the door to open it.
A faint voice hails him: "Christ is risen!"
He leaps to another door. Again,
a faint voice hails him: "Christ is risen!"
By way of a third door he seeks to flee.
A third voice hails him: "Christ is risen!"
In ghostly silence, the three doors move,
opening and shutting of themselves.

Behold! three forms, like brothers, weird, forlorn,
each holding a blown-out Easter candle.
They follow his fleeing, despairing footsteps
wherever he turns, wherever he goes.
The Easter clothes they wear
are stained, flapping, torn;
the moving rags surround him,
before and behind the choir-stalls.

Not once in his flight can he outdistance them.
Here and there, front and back, above, below,
eight feet touch the flagstones together.
All of them run but only his are heard.
With long strides in vain he tries
to flee the footsteps from Hell,
like a summer star which shoots down
swiftly for five or ten fathoms.

Thirty times they circle
the echoing church together,
the smell of incense fills the church,
as if forty censers are burning!
Ever they run in swift pursuit and ever
the live man leads the wretched phantoms.
They bend, confer in secret for long;
the funeral cotton moves; it almost falls from their mouths.

Ah! Whoever saw the Virgin Mary
lifting her hands to close her eyes?
Ah! Whoever at Easter saw Christ
sweating blood, everything reddening?
What a weight of evil oppresses the church
that this very day resounded
with so many joys and psalms,
flooded in light.

He finds himself before the Holy Altar.
He shudders, kneels before the three.
In horror he stares and calls to them:
"I know you! What is your wish? You are my sons!
Each of your faces resembles mine.
Only say, why do you haunt my steps?
Forgive and desist. Leave me in peace.

It is not yet the Advent of Christ.
O damned ones, unloose my hands."

Then their lips they glued to his;
and the kisses they gave were each a knife
that pierced the wretch's heart.
Since the stars first shed their rays on earth,
such kisses of horror were never bestowed.
He spat to expel the poison from his lips,
but the funeral cotton had entered within.

He stood like a marble pillar till dawn,
and the dead boys had vanished.
Slow and fearful, he lifted his head
and inhaled the heavy incense of the dead.
At last his wild eyes fixed themselves
on the laurels. Time passed and then he said:
"Go, sign of Joy." And he filled his fists
with laurels and flung them at the Cross.

"Truly there is a hell. I believe it. It spreads
and all of it burns in my vitals.
Tonight a capricious Being
sent me my sons from their graves;
and yesterday, unknown to me,
He thrust my daughter into my arms.
Nothing remains now but for Him
to destroy Himself, for He created me."

He rises and takes to the plain; he crashes
through forests and valleys, mountains and ravines;
In his eyes the green grass is black,
the waters and trees are black.
He rushes forth madly,
and though his eyes see only blackness,

he thinks he still is pursued,
he still feels the cotton of death in his mouth.

Thus when murderers, evildoers
seek to close their eyes in sleep,
the secretly murdered drenched in blood,
come all together and step on his breast.
Naked, he cries aloud for help;
from his warm bed he leaps
and his thoughts are so black,
that wide-eyed he sees the murdered before him.

MARIA'S DREAM (from LAMBROS)

In my dream I seem to be
sailing on the deserted sea;
I struggle alone with winds and wave.
You are not near me;
In my danger, I see nothing
but the sky;
I look at it, "Help me," I say. "I have
no sail or rudder, yet I sail the sea."

Then, as I say these words,
see, three boys leap in of a sudden,
The wood creaks so from their weight,
it seems the boat will break asunder.
Then death appears inevitable.
Huddled together they talk in secret,
and once they have said their secret words,
with broken oars they row the boat.

With a bitter smile on her lips
a girl appears and comes toward me;

her body is wrapped in a shroud
that billows white in the wind,
but even paler is the color
of the hand she raises before me,
and it trembles, as the reed trembles,
when she shows me the cross on her palm.

And I see blood running from the cross,
black blood gushing like a fountain;
the girl casts a troubled glance at me,
that seems to say she cannot aid me.
The more the oars tear through the storm,
the more the current swells around me;
again and again the lightning splits the darkness,
and the thunder crashes on.

Sometimes the waves hurl us high in the air,
till it seems we are up in the clouds,
and sometimes they sink so despairingly
that we fear hell is gaping before us.
The oarsmen turn to face me;
they hurl maledictions: "May you be damned!"
The sea leaps over us
and the whole boat sinks.

While I struggle hard with hands and feet
in that storm that opens my grave for me
and never lets me raise
my head above the wave, I find myself
wretched and prone on the bed
that so often sin has warmed.
I weep most bitterly, for the wall is
bare of the wedding wreath you promised.

JULIUS TYPALDOS

1814-1883. Born in Cephalonia. He studied law in Italy. A contemporary of Dionysios Solomos for whom he had an almost fanatic admiration. He returned to the Ionian Islands in 1839 and taught at Corfu. He went back to Italy and continued his studies at Padua, Florence and Pisa. He translated many works from the Italian, among which is a large part of Free Jerusalem *by Tasso. He returned to Greece and was elected judge of Cephalonia, Corfu and Zante. In 1862 he became Supreme Judge. Like Solomos, Typaldos was an ardent champion of the vernacular. He died in Corfu.*

THE EXECUTION OF THE KLEPHT

"Farewell high mountains and crystalline springs,
refreshing dawns and moonlit nights,
swarthy young klephts, terror of the Turks!
No illness smites me, yet I go to my death;
when the bullet strikes my body, yet my soul will live;
I shall become a small black bird, a small black swallow,
coming with the sweet dawn to see where you are fighting.
And when the battle ends, and the pale moon rises,
again I will come to stand by a small cypress,
to lament for the few klephts I shall find on earth;
in the solitude of night, while they are sleeping;
so their mothers will hear me and keen them a dirge.
See the gate of the Pasha! I had better stop my song.
Farewell high mountains, flowing streams;
Brothers, bury me on a high hill,
that I may hear nightingales ushering in April,
and when they bring out the frankincense with the *Christ is*
from Saint Sophia, the great basilica,   [*Risen,*

I shall become a white bird and fly to Constantinople,
I shall sing sweetly like a bird of paradise!"
He had barely said these words when he fell down dead.
On the spot where they buried him a cypress has grown,
and each sweet dawn when the May breeze blows,
a lonely bird perches on a lonely cypress tree.
He looks eastward, toward Constantinople,
and he sings a sad and plaintive song.

ARISTOTELIS VALAORITIS

1824-1879. Born at Lefkas. He studied abroad. He traveled to Italy, Switzerland, Scotland, Germany, Hungary. In 1857, he was elected a member of the Ionian Parliament, and in 1862, a member of the Athenian Parliament. Valaoritis regarded the demotic klephtic songs as his models. His first volume of poetry appeared in 1845. His complete works were published in 1891. Most important of his works are Photinos *(a poem never completed),* Athanase Diakos *(1867),* Kyra Phrosini *(1859). Valaoritis played an important political role in the Greek struggle for liberation. His work is mostly of a patriotic nature. Some of his most successful poems are about the Greek War of Independence. His* Ode to Patriarch Gregorios *is studied in almost all schools.*

PHOTINOS THE PLOWMAN (excerpt of a poem never completed)

. . . .

Out of the black fog comes a rider
and halts his horse before the plowman . . .

. . . .

"Did you stone my two grey-hounds,
foul old peasant?"
    "I alone and no one else."
"Speak to me more humbly . . . bow your head,
worship your master, outcast, beggar!"

. . . .

And the Frank strikes the white hair with a pike.

. . . .

"You knew all the while those dogs were mine?"
"I knew and I drove them out of my seed bed."

"Where do you come from?"
    "From here . . . Sphakissa."

"And am I an unknown worm, I, George Gratianos,
your tyrant, your lord, master in perpetuity?
This earth on which I stand, the stones, the streams,
tame and wild branch, the breeze, your very soul,
your livestock, children, your blood, your honor,
all are mine, know it. Wild beast of mountain, ravine,
furred or feathered, the loathsome carrion,
the migrating bird, belong only to me,
and your head is worth less than a tiny hare or partridge.
That is why my dogs and I will pass whenever I please,
you own nothing and the seedbed here is mine.
And you deserve no better fate. Accursed, of a cowardly race,
creature old and wretched that lives still in the world,
only to shame his name and his descendants!"

. . . .

With the last words, the plowman felt a tear
wetting the white of his eye,
and all the hair of his body stirred.

. . . .

"Though the branch be dry, its root is green.
Cattle like me always cling to life whether they eat pome-
                                                  [granate or rye.
And though cattle like me can bellow loudly,
yet easily are they roused by the prick of a fly and whirl about,
and they are called the People. One day the worm
will break the chains and appear with wings,
then who knows how high the crawling bird will fly!" . . .

"Show me this corpse that will haunt us."

"I . . . poor Photinos, the old man, the ragman,
who plant my seed here for you to take;

ARISTOTELIS VALAORITIS

I, who knead the soil with my sweat
for another to eat bread; who run and graft
the mountain olive tree, who have no oil
to light my candle and who live in hell.
I, who with my nails turn upside down
ravines and boulders to deck them for you
with vineyards, who do not reap, who never have
a little juicy wine to wet my tongue.
I, the poor miller, whose head is always spinning,
who take as pay and profit, the leavings for my bread;
who do not own my son, who always live in terror
and who can find no law on earth to judge for me.
I—I am the People, the soulless corpse,
the draught ox, the dead ram . . .
Do not load his burdened back any more . . ."

. . . .

"Hold your serpent tongue, peasant.
Do not stir my bile again. Kneel
and ask for mercy, for my grey-hounds . . .
Rebel, you refuse! Do you not hear?"
    "I would rather hang
than bend my knees . . . else would I be accursed.
They would make deep hollows and it would be a great sin,
to bury name and honor in such a grave."

ATHANASE DIAKOS (excerpt—fourth song)

(a lay priest who had turned klepht and fought for liberty)

The Albanians still sleep, glutted, weary
in the dense verdure. So many thousands of people,
and not one sweet dream, not a single heart-throb!

No hopes shine in the cloud of their sleep,
no distant desire. Gloom is in their eyes,
desolation in their hearts. The human flocks
are silent from exhaustion, dozing
among the April flowers, dark heaps lying
as if they were fragments, moss-covered rocks
thrown by destruction from some high tower,
sown here and there by the hand of the earthquake.
The Pleiades still swing high and the morning cock
has not yet crowed. Before the crescent moon
slides down the slope of the mountain crest,
it stops for a moment and, embittered, casts
a last glance on deserted Zitouni.
The ravines darken. Within the inky wave
the breeze drowns the crops, the trees, the meadows;
the dry land becomes a sea; it seems this night
has come with two midnights, and it takes long to dawn.

In the dense darkness the millenial oak
menaced the sky with its wild rage.
Proud spirit of earth that aspired to reach
the clouds with its branches and Hell with its root,
it did not perceive how time the destroyer
had nested in its heart and dug a cavity
gnawing slowly, slowly with its teeth.

No gay flower had ever sprouted
under its heavy shadow. Nor did the camomile
or wild cyclamen. All around it mullein
and poisonous vines. Here and there in the soil
scattered shoulder bones, whose flesh the dog's tooth
had torn or the raven's claws,
rotted, unburied. And if some lost soul
passed there and heard the moths
sawing sleeplessly the hollow joints

and all night long grinding, he made his cross
and did not even turn to look at the frightful tree.
In its black hollow lived a solitary gypsy,
an old man, tattered, mute, sun-scorched,
off-spring of small-pox, last child of leprosy.
Disease grazed deep within him, mowed down his vitals,
a hidden neverending enmity for the flowers, the stars,
the child's beauty, and he devoured with the eye
whatever his hard hand could not reach to corrupt.
He wore his corruption stretched out on the rags,
brought to him each time by thefts, the noose.
His inseparable comrades were hammers, ropes, the anvil,
flints for flaying, rusty nails, shears,
one bat, one scorpion, a magpie, a turtle.
No one in Livadia knew whence he had come.
Did a cloud drop him? . . . Did the soil of the oak
vomit him? . . . No one knows.
When at night on the grindstone, he ground the tools,
and moved his hands and shook his head,
(an unnatural growth on the belly of the tree)
from afar he appeared like an immense
octopus in its lair awaiting its prey,
and flailing uneasily with its tentacles.

Diakos is buried in this hollow since last night;
the lightning of the mountain burnt out in his grave.
Joyfully the spider holds him in its clutches
and sucks his soul. The gypsy strews dry shavings
in the cave and casts Diakos over them.
He unhinges his arms with tongs, with a rope,
he weights them with iron. He binds his feet,
squeezes his neck in a vise. He presses his chest
with a sharp cornerstone. He charms reptiles
and shakes them over him. Then, cross-legged,

the murderer watches them lest they sleep
and leave unfinished their nocturnal deeds.

But the eye of God also keeps watch.

KERA PHROSINI (excerpt—second song)

The wind carries me on its wings
like a withered yellow leaf
far from you, tormented.
Phrosini, love me while I am in exile.

The motionless wave on the shore
slept sweetly, a deep sleep;
the North Wind blew and a storm
hurled the wave on the rocks to be dashed.

Phrosini, they are sending me to strange lands
to go to war, to the firing line.
Offer me from your loving lips,
a thousand kisses to accompany me.

If my day has come, my soul, my heart,
for foreign earth, foreign birds
to drink my blood, gnaw at my heart,
in the desert, greedily,

my love, who knows, your kisses
may give me life to be reborn,
to come like a dream into your arms,
Phrosini, poor me, to sleep.

Winter is coming, clouds, snows,
flowers and fragrance have fled;
the swallows, Phrosini dear, have gone,
beware, black nights are over us.

The rapacious hawk, the mean sparrow hawk
will begin to prey all around.
My soul, woe to the pigeon if the hawk
should find it alone in its nest.

Phrosini, they are sending me to foreign lands,
to go to war, to the firing line.
Who knows what fate has in store for me;
my soul, Phroso dear, good-bye.

THE CREEPING VINE

The thickly blossomed creeping vine tells
the monstrous plane tree facing her,
often shadowing her,
always over her evening and dawn:

"Proud tree, your leaves and boughs
shake wildly in the breeze;
now do you find the earth narrow,
are not the stars, the clouds spacious enough for you?

"Cool water trickles at your roots,
you suckle the mist easily,
and you, so mighty, are jealous of me,
because I can get a little freshness.

"What do you want, plane tree, what do you seek from me?
Remove your shadow, for I am small.
My flowers are frozen, do not torment them,
let my share of sunshine bring them joy . . ."

"My yellow-haired creeping vine, why do you fear me?
Do you want always to creep, an orphan,
by yourself, desolate in the night,
sleeping on a stone, the bare earth?

"Mate your flowers with my manhood,
become a queen and I the throne,
cling to me . . . in my arms,
every other flower will envy you . . ."

The wild plane tree ensnared her,
entwined her among the twigs.
What a pity, yellow-haired plant, you gave up
your virginity to raise yourself a little.

Poor and unmarried, in your loneliness,
your flowers were my secret joy;
now, my lady, the clouds and the wind
will steal your fragrance.

GERASIMOS MARKORAS

1826-1911. Born in Cephalonia. He traveled to Italy, studied law in Ionian Academy but dedicated himself to letters. He was a friend and disciple of Dionysios Solomos. Kostes Palamas held him in high esteem for his sense of harmony and impeccability of form. The Oath (1876) is an epic which consists of 1800 lines and relates to the Cretan Revolution of 1866. Poetic Works appeared in 1890. Little Journeys (1890). Palamas wrote a critical essay on Markoras (1913).

TWO

Two of us are left! Who knows what the book
of Fate has in store for us next,
which will be first to go to sunless places,
which of us will be left alone.

Since the stern will of God has ordered
that we live, wretched, childless, and old
let each hold the hand of the other
till it feels insensible, cold.

Such a joy—let us covet no other—
in the ardent affection that burned us,
is, sister, a great consolation.

Ah! The day when this too has stopped,
if the world sheds only one tear,
let it mourn the living, not the other.

INNOCENT FEARS

Child: I want mama.
Father: She flew away and went to live among the stars.
Child: How could a sick woman have the strength to tear through so much space?
Father: Souls have wings.
Child: Then why don't our souls spread their wings too so she won't be running alone after the stars.
Father: She isn't alone. Angels flap their wings all around her.
Child: But if she used to call me angel, she must want me near her.
Father: Oh! Without an invitation from God, no one goes to heaven. Sleep now. Rest.
Child: And who is going to sing to me?
Father: I, my little son.
Child: You weep.
Father: No, lean on me! *May your sleep be sugar and your dream be honey.*
Child: I am sleepy. Do not ever move from my side. Give me your hand. I am afraid you may fly away too.

A DEAD MAIDEN'S COMPLAINT

Lovely world, how ardently
I hold you now in my heart!
I even hear your April breeze
deep in my grave.

Would it were possible, O God,
with all that grows
from the earth girdling me
to come forth like a rose!

Before death dragged me
to flowerless deserts,
I saw such a festival
fourteen times.

Unlucky me, I had barely
started my sweet communion
with the air, the fountain,
the green boughs.

The flowers, the grass,
the crowd of stars of heaven,
told my heart a story
my mind could not fathom.

The dawn had assumed
a new beauty in my eyes,
and the moon awoke in me
a thousand secret feelings.

In blossomy or wild haunts,
sauntering alone,
"Who," I asked, "Who can
explain what I feel?"

Then I saw
the answer written
on a gracious face
in an angelic eye,

but before the voice could speak
to me clearly, freely,
Death swooped down like a hawk
and cast me here.

That memory weighs on me
as heavily as the earth.

Would that I could fly high up
like a swallow from the other world!

O dear Christ! Let me live again,
only as long as I need,
to be able to know
the great secret of my heart.

From SPRING NIGHTS

The ocean laughs. The moon
silvers it on its way to the west;
you'd think this is why it swells with joy
without a breeze to help it.

In such sweetness, what is the sorrow
that suddenly conquers me without reason,
and wars to conceal from my eyes
each magic of the silent night?

All around is quiet. Loving night,
are you going to remind me, an old man,
with such a falling asleep of nature,
what sleep I am about to find in hell?

In such an hour, when no cloud
conceals its face,
happy is the man who hopes for heaven,
to match the last hour of his life with this.

I hope for it; though somehow I foresee
that I will close my eyes in peace,
Ah! I am loath to quit the lovely world
laughing before me.

GEORGIOS VIZINOS

1849-1896. Born in Thrace. He studied in Athens and later in Germany. He published Kodros, My Life's Journey, Moscov Selim, Ares Manes Koukounares, Breeze of Bosphorus, Attic Breeze *and a novel entitled* My Mother's Sin, *written and published in Paris, in Greek and in French. He composed ballads inspired by the demotic songs but written in the manner of Schiller.*

THE DREAM

Last night in my sleep, I saw
a deep river,
God forbid
that the dream come true!
On its shore stood a lad,
someone I knew,
pale as the moon,
silent as the night.

The wind pushed him with violence,
with a mighty strength,
as if it wanted to drive him
from the midst of life.
And the water, greedily
kissing his feet,
seemed to invite him
to plunge within its embrace.

It is not the wind, I thought,
that lashes you too.
Despair seizes you,
and the world's cruelty!

And I rushed forth to snatch
the wretch from death . . .
Ah me! Before I reached him,
he was lost from my sight!

I leaned out into the stream
I tried to find him.
There in the water,
I saw the fresh corpse! . . .
Last night in my sleep, I saw
a deep river.
God forbid,
that the dream come true!

THE HIDDEN SORROW

My friends will never be able to say
that I hide what little joy I know.
The quick wings of my song
strew it among my companions,
unblemished and clear.
But no one, no one will learn
of the sorrow flooding
the depths of my heart.

The whole world is not indifferent.
I say this in praise.
But each man has so many sorrows,
he barely finds time
to cheer himself.
That is why no one will learn
of the sorrow flooding
the depths of my heart.

Once I saw a good woman,
sadder than the rest of us.
Had she known my heart was pining,
she would have flown
to sweetly console me.
She would have understood
the sorrow flooding
the depths of my heart.

But she has left for a faraway land
where news cannot reach her!
Ah! my sweet lady is dead—
they have buried her
within the frozen earth!
That is why no one, no one will learn
of the sorrow flooding
the depths of my heart.

ALEXANDROS PALLIS

1851-1941. Born at Piraeus. At the age of 18 he left Greece for England. From there he went to India as a merchant, then returned to Liverpool where he spent many years. One of the most militant defenders of the demotic, he translated The New Testament *into the vernacular which caused riots on the streets of Athens. He also translated* The Iliad *(Liverpool 1920) into the vernacular, in verse. In 1924 he published a book of travel impressions entitled* Brusos. *He translated a part of Kant's* Critique of Pure Reason. *These last two are to be found in a collection entitled* Rotten Walnuts. *He translated into the vernacular* The Cyclops *of Euripides and Shakespeare's* Merchant of Venice. *He edited* Antigone. *He translated the first book of Thucydides with critical notes. He collected more than 550 pages from ancient Greek, English and French which he translated into the demotic.*

GIRL FROM ROUMELY

I envy that village
in the valley below
with its tall belfry
its church,
with the Virgin Mary
in silver and gold.
Rinio often goes there
to kiss her.

I envy that village
in the valley below
with the deep fields,
its trees

heavy with olives,
kissing the earth
and glistening
like Rinio's black eyes.

I envy that village
in the valley below
with its branches
blossomy, breathing fragrance,
every vineyard
with rosy grapes,
dripping honey
like Rinio's soft lips.

I envy that village
in the valley below
with its limpid springs,
its streams.
The waters scatter life . . .
Rinio, please,
come too, with a little love,
to bring me life.

KANARIS

(Greek naval hero and statesman in the period of the Greek War of Independence who burnt the Turkish fleet just outside the island of Chios.)

The whole assembly of elders gathered at the pier agreed
they would wait for the Turks on the mainland.
Then I took off my fez,
and coming forward to the center, I made bold to say:

"Gentlemen, nothing but ships can save us."
Immediately one of our mighty bigwigs heard, he flared up
[and poured out his venom:
"Who is this man, and what is his name, who dares to advise
[us?"
This is how Psara was lost. And I took the torch in my hand,
and headed for Chios,
and I shouted from there—I couldn't help it—with bitter lips:
"Hear me! Now you will know my name!"

WOMAN FROM SAMOS

Tell me widow up there on the terrace
robustly dressed in your island breeches,
with your fez tilted on your head,
and the full white bloomers,

why do you stupidly chase the girls
as they circle about you laughing, teasing?
Widow, perhaps you too often see,
leaping upon you with open arms,

some gallant young man in your dreams.
And now, tell me widow, does he seize you
and melt you with his kisses,
or, wretched one, do you awake too soon?

KOSTES PALAMAS

1859-1943. Born in Patras but lived in Missolonghi. From the age of three, he lived in Athens. Palamas dedicated his life to the cause of the demotic language. In 1881-1887 he was occupied with journalism. He contributed regularly to the newspapers Akropolis, Ephemeris *and the magazine* Estia. *He introduced to Greeks the great Ionian writers: Calvos, Typaldos, Markoras, Kalosgouros, Laskaratos and Mavilis. In 1897 Palamas joined in the language fight between Vlachos and Rhoidis. In 1897, too, he was appointed Secretary of the University, a post which he kept until his death. A prolific writer, his poetic works are:* Songs of My Country *(1886),* Hymn to Athene *(1889),* The Eyes of My Soul *(1892),* Iambs and Anapests *(1897),* The Grave *(1898),* Greetings of the Sun-Born *(1900),* The Death of the Young Man *(novel) (1901),* Trisevgene (Royal Blossom—*a drama) (1903),* Life Immovable *(1904),* Helen of Sparta *(translation of Emile Verhaeren's work) (1904),* Letters *(1904 and 1907),* The Twelve Songs of the Gypsy *(1907),* The King's Flute *(1910),* City and Solitude *(1912),* The Lagoon's Regrets and the Satires *(1912),* First Critical Papers *(1913),* The Altars *(first series 1915),* Poems Out of Season *(1919),* Sonnets *(1919),* Dekatetrasticha *(1919),* Tales *(1920),* The Pentasyllables and Pathetic Whispers *(1925),* Verses Mild and Harsh *(1928—published in America),* The Cycle of Tetrastichs *(1928),* Passings and Greetings *(1931),* Criticism, First Series *(1894),* Studies in Literature Vol. 1 *(1907),* Studies in Literature Vol. 2 *(1911),* Music Reaccented *(1930),* Heroic Persons and Events *(1913), Palamas was twice nominated for the Nobel Prize.*

ROSE-FRAGRANCE (from CITY AND SOLITUDE)

This year the heavy winter hit me hard;
it caught me without fire, it found me without youth,
and from hour to hour, I expected to crumple, a heap
on the snow-covered road . . .

But yesterday, as the laughter of March cheered me,
and I went ahead to find once more the ancient lanes,
at the first fragrance of a faraway rose
my eyes filled with tears.

THE FATHERS (from THE ALTARS)

Child, do not neglect the garden you inherit.
No matter how you find it, how it seems to you,
dig it even deeper, fence it more securely,
enrich its flowers; widen its earth,
prune it where it tangles unpruned,
carry pure water from the fountainhead,
and if you love life and what is not ill,
pour holy water and exhort the evil spirits to go.
Plant its aliveness with all that is sound, fresh;
be a plowman, planter, guardian;
and if lean years come, hard times befall,
and frightened birds leave and the many trees
serve only as parapets,
do not fear destruction. Fire! The Axe! Go,
uproot it, let the garden lie fallow, clear it,
build a fort upon it and entrench yourself within,
for battling, for bleeding, for the new age
which we always await, which always tries to arrive,

and is always lost, a fragment, at the turn of the cycles.
It is enough that an idea guides you, commands you,
an idea worn like a crown, sharp as a sword, dominating all.

THE GRAVE (excerpt)

On the voyage where
the Black Horseman leads you,
be wary, from his hand
take nothing he gives you.

And if you thirst, drink not
from the world below
the water of oblivion,
poor cut mint, no more to grow.

Do not drink and forget me
completely as day follows day,
set up your guide-posts
not to lose the way.

And since you are light
as the swallow small,
and no warrior's arms
clang at your belt at all,

try to outwit
the sultan of night,
glide slowly, in secret;
then fly to the light.

And returning, my dearest,
to our grief-stricken home,
be light as the zephyr,
your kiss like the foam.

THE TWELVE SONGS OF THE GYPSY

(This is an epic poem in twelve parts about the Gypsies, their arrival in Thrace, and their later settlement in Constantinople. The Gypsy (the poet), of the poem sings of his people and their carefree life.)

> "And I felt within me, that I too was a gypsy, no matter how much I was ashamed to reveal it—a gypsy with his evil ways and his evil fate."
> Prologue—*Twelve Songs of the Gypsy*

The Arrival (first song—excerpt)

The dense darknesses
were streaked by a line of white
very like night.
It was my mind's first
dawning.

Honey-sweet was the hour.
Everything was filled
with something more caressing
than the gentle breeze
wafting morning balsam
of the evergreen pines
and the gentle breeze.
It was somewhere in a land,
a source of peoples and ages
in Thrace.

It was where two opposing peoples
with the same lustful mania
yearn to embrace
the lovely unique Bosporus.

In colorful dress they set up camp;
they kissed the earth
where the city's feet walked.
All peoples thronged there like locusts;
they swarmed there like bees,
for she was queen of two shores,
a Nereid fashioned of foam,
and this was you, Constantinople,
O Constantinople!

This was the garden of the world,
where peoples met from distant poles
in a single blaze of glory,
where from the ends of the world,
inharmonious strangers
fought in Rome of the Constantines,
under the labarum
of the Greeks.

And between the banks of the Straits
it was as if cities of green
were growing.
A fountain of young shoots sprouted,
the flowers were like phantoms,
shed from on high,
a rain of rubies
into golden reservoirs.

And the sun beat down
from the mountains of Bithynia
on Magnavras and Blachernas.
And these palaces reflecting
all the brilliance of the sun,
raised their proud domes
disdainfully on high.

And from the Golden Gates of the forts,
from the impregnable Seven Towers,
to the ends of the scattered emerald islands,
were legions of palaces,
and armies of monastaries.

LOVE (third song—excerpt)

Partridge-breasted Gypsy,
enchantress, you speak
a commanding language
to the stars at midnight.

As you speak, you loom gigantic,
leaving worlds behind,
and the stars place on you
a fairy crown!

Tighten round me the clasp
of your masterful hands;
I am love's sorcerer,
you, the enchantress of the stars.

THE FAIR OF KAKAVA (seventh song excerpt)

Gypsies came wearing
gaudy holiday costumes,
gypsies came with strings of thick,
glittering beads round their necks.
They came in red dresses,
with long yellow kerchiefs.
O wanton eyes, breasts, lips!

They came with flowers in their hair,
all the blossoms of May.
And holding flowers in their hands
they strike tambourines and bells.
They weave circles and they dance
and sing a song of May.
And one of them,
a girl of eighteen, steps out
from amidst her companions
and starts a tempestuous dance.
She sways, crouches, leaps,
in the delirium of the dance,
she is queen of the dance,
light as foam, languorous, palpitating,
the young Gypsy girl, queen of the May!

THE PROPHET (eighth song—excerpt)

And a day will come, a black day!
And your soul, O State
will filter, drop by drop
far, far over the proud land,
while the sun shines bright,
the April breezes blow.
And the light, frightening the sun,
as if fed by your own blood,
will rise a mockery, a depravity, a deception,
a wailing, a Kingdom.

See your two-headed eagle! It flew far,
far with the holy and the true,
and its vast wings will cast their shadow
on other peoples, other peaks, other slopes.

Westward and northward
it carries and clasps the crown
of glory and might
in its rapacious claws.
And the mockery, deception, the kingdom,
born of you within the sun,
O God, see! It will lie low before
a stuffed owl.
It will live with all your baseness,
with none of your greatness,
and the prophets it will worship
will be pygmies and clowns.
And its wise men, its judges,
will be victors of the empty word;
its protectors,
its governors will be eunuchs.

And you will shun the corrupt body,
oh soul tormented by sin,
and the body will not find a palm's width
of earth to use as a grave,
and the carcass will lie unburied,
for dogs and reptiles to devour,
and in its cycles, Time will guard
the memory of some sorry skeleton.

Finally the god of love
will pity you,
and a dawn will break
and the voice of redemption will call you,
O soul tormented by sin!
You will hear the deliverer's voice;
you will strip off the dress of sin,
and once more self-governed and free,
you will stir like the grass, the bird,

like the breast of woman, the wave.
There will be no step below this
that can roll you down
the ladder of Evil.
You will feel the joy spreading—
your wings,
your first wide wings
for the ascent that summons you!

THE SATYR or THE SONG OF NUDITY

Nudity is everywhere—
here all is bare,
fields, mountains, horizons.
The day is unrestrained,
Nature is diaphanous,
deep palaces wide open;
eyes, fill yourselves with light,
guitars with rhythm.

Here the trees are sparse,
ill-seeming blots to the eye;
the world is pure wine.
Nudity is queen.
Here shadow is a dream,
there even dawns
in night's misty mouth
an amber smile.

Here nature's breast is free,
raging without shame;
the bare rock is a star;
the body a flame.

Your divine nudity
O thrice-noble Attica,
offers rubies, gold,
pearls, silver!

Here youth is magic,
the flesh glorified.
Virgins are huntress-queens,
desires, quicksilver gods.
Here every hour is naked.
Wondrous to sea-monsters,
Aphrodite rises on the billows
and rules everywhere.

Strip your garments,
and invest yourself with nudity.
Soul, priestess of nudity,
your body is a temple.
Let my hands be magnets—
amber toward the flesh.
Let me drink of nudity
the nectar of the gods.

Tear off your veil, throw away
your unbecoming chiton.
Let your plastic image
blend with nature.
Loosen your girdle, cross
your hands on your breast;
let your damson hair
be a long-trained gown.

Be an immobile statue;
let your body acquire
the perfection of art,
gleaming on the stone;

perform with idea's nudity
and play the role
of supple beasts,
serpents, birds.

Perform and play the role
of the voluptuous and lovely;
refine your nudity
and mould the idea.
The rounded, the straight,
youthful hair, lines, curves,
O divine tremors,
join in a dance.

Brow, eyes, waves of hair,
buttocks and loins,
secret gorges of love,
roses, myrtles, secret places,
feet that you chain,
fountains of caress, O hands,
doves of desire,
vultures of doom!

And heartfelt, unfettered
words, O mouth, O mouth,
like the wax of bees,
like the hue of the rose.
The alabaster lilies,
censers of April,
envy your breast.
Oh! Let me drink from your breast.

To sip from your rose-printed,
high-enameled breasts
the milk of happiness
of this I dreamed . . .

I am your hierophant;
your knees are altars;
in your fiery embrace,
the gods perform prodigies.

Far from us the indecorous,
the draped and the covered,
the hated and ugly,
unclean and strange.
All upright, nude, guileless,
earth, air, bodies, breasts.
Truth is also nudity;
nudity is beauty.

In the sun-burst radiance
of an Athenian day,
if there appears before you
a creature like a bare monster,
like a leafless tree,
without the virtue of shade,
a crude stone,
a spare body,

a creature nude, uncovered,
on the open expanse
which only two fiery eyes
show to have life,
something from the Satyr world,
and it is a beast,
its voice is silver,
do not flee. It is I,
the Satyr. My roots are here,
like the olive tree.
I make the winds languish
with my shrill-sounding flute.
I play and they mate,

in love they love others,
I play and they dance,
men, beasts and spirits.

THE DEAD YOUTH (from LIFE IMMOVABLE)

In here, I feel the soul of someone dead,
and the corpse is a blonde—beardless boy.
And a strange yellow light flickers in the house,
days and moments pass, ages and years.
And in his house the soul of the dead
is like the bitter calm around a ship
longing for sea-routes and dreaming of storms.
The faces of all are faces blurred as if
from the funeral tapers and the eyes of all
are eyes fixed on the coffin,
and the lips quiver slowly, shedding
the bitter poison of the last kiss.
Hands are uplifted as if in prayer,
and the feet move as if following
a corpse; and the all-white bareness of the walls,
the abundance of jet-black clothes,
is a music of separate instruments.
The children walk on tip-toe, as if fearful
lest they disturb the sleep of the dead, and the old
always bent as if at the edge of some grave,
lean on the shoulders of maids,
well-meaning, consoling Fates;
and the young men in endless reading, seek
the herb of oblivion from the hands of Wisdom.
And on the shut casement window sills
the flowers in the pots are like funeral offerings,
and the ray gliding through the crack

becomes an All Soul's Day taper.
The candle at the icon flickers
and its sputtering is like a struggle with Death,
and now and then a multi-colored butterfly
poising lightly on the flesh, brings greeting
from the soul that had enchanted the house . . .
Ah, how the house of mourning loved him, how it yearned
to keep the dead boy, the blonde young man!
to hold its dearest treasure,
the house transformed itself into a tomb.

THE LABORERS

We are the laborers who water the earth
with our sweat for it to grow
fruit, flowers, the world's goodness all around us;
only labor is barren, bears no flower or fruit.

We are the laborers who knead
the world's bread with our sweat;
our hands are stronger than swords;
though chained, they dig and the earth grows rich.

Worker, the corrupting laws of this world,
shamelessly let hoarders devour your wealth.
Unite brothers, awake! with one heart, one mind!
Justice, thunder! Progress, flash lightning!

HYMN TO PASSION

It was the hour when all grows dark
and tender. The door opened . . .

You were dressed as the flower
of the pomegranate

is dressed in purple. As you moved
lightly, the silk
that held you softly covered
rustled sweetly,

as if accompanying the song
your body sang to me,
it added mystic grace
unto your music,

and it was as if its restless motion
held a secret summons
for preying passion to set limed twigs
for the wretched man.

I am not certain which is your beauty,
your body or your soul,
what power in your being
draws me to you.

I am not certain which is your beauty.
Are you a grace or a muse,
well-being or disease,
golden-haired girl?

You may be an impulse, an idea,
the language of divine reason,
or the flesh and the temptation
of sin.

I know you breathed within me
as an evening wind blows
beating into the weariness
of a misty day.

Though I may be the weariness of a dim day,
though you may be the evening wind,
you startled from its sleep within me
a monster passion.—

A passion that mingles
some April with the winter,
and thus, a love, I think is shaped
like a mermaid.

A mermaid love, with the face of innocence,
with warm caresses in its eyes,
a mermaid love,—body of a woman
with a fish tail.

See the magnificent story
in the eyes of my fancy;
though it is a scarecrow, though it presses
like a nightmare on my chest.

I sail on dream-oceans.
The ship sails, I stand at the prow,
the water-nymph, angry spirit of the sea,
blocks my path.

She is a dragon huntress in hot pursuit
of the gluttonous desire of man,
a question always inexorably on her lips
for one to fathom.

Can he who answers
her question be saved?
I do not know except that one is doomed,
remaining silent before her.

Mermaid love on the waves where
I sail with my heart, mind, soul,

your asking is vain; I cannot answer,
you may drown me!

You were dressed as the pomegranate
flower is dressed in purple;
a hammer thuds upon my heart
as it blazes on the anvil,

a hammer pounds on my heart
as it blazes on the anvil to fashion it
—of what metal?—into a wreath
for your golden hair.

I thought my pale lips would lean
to kiss your flower-hands . . .
But how quickly you recoiled
as if knives had touched you!

Your shrinking, lightning withdrawal,
almost caused a harsh separation,
like a river parting two banks
that would have touched.

Then angrily, with a Satyr's violence,
I thought against your will
to stretch over you my cold hands,
to warm them on your knees,

or even lustfully with the impulse
of the beast to lunge wildly,
to trample on the uncondescending,
cut lilies.

To trample on the uncondescending,
cut lilies of your youth as
the reveler smashes the glass
of the wine he has gulped.

But ah! the storm-cloud has vanished
rapidly in the azure depths of the dream!
And oh the Satyr's fingers cling fast,
held to his flute.

And the Satyr's fingers are rough
and all his motions! All spins around me.
Around your boughs my care flits
like a butterfly.

Around us, myriad spirits
of centuries past, all inter-twined
sleep lightly in books
earthly and divine,

as if they were waiting for hands and eyes
to awaken them, summon them
to celebrate loves,
mystic weddings.

For even though all, centuries old
sleep lightly, diffused around us,
in books mundane and divine,
they surely have us in mind.

For they see both you and me
in their living pages
with serenity stirred
by a shudder

as when a breeze ripples,
a spreading thoughtful sea,
without enraging foamy waters
and black waves.

For my people are your people
and suckled on the same milk,

we delve into study
and start on voyages.

But further on is a life, another life,
the wedding of earth and ether,
the day shining with all her light,
all her magic.

But though we were moved by spirits
air-bound by the same thread,
within you the blood seethed
with the flame of youth.

And though we were moved
air-bound by the same chain,
thought seized me again; and I saw you
in a pitch-black deep.

And you were dressed as the pomegranate
flower is dressed in purple.
A hammer thuds on my heart
as it blazes on the anvil,

a hammer pounds my heart
as it blazes on the anvil to shape it
like the hair on your forehead
into a golden wreath.

And I told my pale lips:—"Pale lips,
do not kiss her flower-hands!
Under her shade, I am as I am
beneath the stars."

Heart that burns and is never
consumed! Destiny so orders it.
Remove your raiment from the flame
under the hammer,

remove your raiment and yourself,
and you, queen in purple,
become the Idea and hymn of passion,
and live, Lyre!

GEORGIOS DROSSINIS

1859—. Born in Athens and lives in Kyphyssia. In 1889 he founded the demotic literary review Estia. *He also founded the magazine* National Education. *He became director of Arts and Literature in the Department of Education. Poetic Works:* Spider Webs *(1880),* Stalactites *(1881),* Idylls *(1884),* Amaranths *(1890),* Calm Time *(1902),* Luminous Darknesses *(1914),* Immortals *(1891),* Closed Eyelids *(1914-1917),* The Sword of Fire and Alconides *(1921), Works in Prose:* Letters of the Fields *(1882),* Short Stories and Remembrances *(1896),* Short Stories *(1889),* Three Days at Tinos *(1883),* Tales of the Fields and City *(1904),* The Plant of Love *(1901),* Amarylis *(1926).* Erse *is a novel.*

GREEK EARTH

Now that I leave for foreign lands,
and we will be parted for months, for years,
let me take something also from you,
dearly beloved, azure land.
Let me carry an amulet with me,
to ward off evil, to ward off grief,
a charm to ward off sadness, death,
a handful of earth, Greek earth!

Earth cooled by nocturnal winds,
earth baptized by the rains of May,
earth scented by the summer seasons,
blessed earth, earth bearing fruit—
the muscat vine, the yellow grain,
the tender laurel, bitter olive,—
through the grace of the Pleiades alone,
through the torrid kisses of the sun.

Honoured earth they dug to lay
the groundwork of the Parthenon!
Glorious earth imbrued with red
by blood of Marathon and Suli!
Earth that buries the warrior dead
of Psara and of Missolonghi,
Earth, that to me too will bring,
courage, joy and pride and glory.

I will hang you—an amulet on my breast,
and when my heart shall wear you as a charm,
it will draw strength and help from you,
lest other alien charms seduce it.
Your loveliness will give me strength,
and wherever I am, wherever I stand,
you will keep alive my deepest yearning—
one day to return to Greece.

And if my fate—dismal and black—
dooms me to leave—never to return,
I will find in you my last forgiveness,
I will give to you my final kiss.
Thus if I die on foreign earth,
the foreign grave will be more sweet,
if you, beloved earth, come with me,
laid on my heart, Greek earth!

THE ALMOND TREE

She shook the flowering almond tree
with tiny hands.
Her back, her arms, her tiny curls
were caped with flowers.

When I saw the silly girl so heaped with snow,
I kissed her sweetly.
I shook the blossoms from her head
and thus I spoke to her:

"Silly girl, why do you hurry to bring
the snowy season to your hair?
Do you not know that the heavy winter
will come of itself?

"Then will you try to see the past in vain,
your little games—
an old lady, tiny, with pure white hair,
with tiny spectacles!"

VESPERS

In the ruined chapel
the divine chisel of Spring
has etched drawings
with the wild flowers of April.

The sun sinking to the west
before the Holy Gate
enters timidly to pray
and lights a brilliant candle.

It scatters a sweet fragrance
laurel rooted in the wall
incense burned by faith

and a nest of swallows built
high in the vestibule
chant 'Glory to God in the Highest.'

LORENZO MAVILIS

1860-1912. Born in Ithaca. He studied philosophy and languages in Athens and in Germany where he spent 14 years in universities. He received his doctorate in 1890 from the University of Bavaria. He translated from English, Sanskrit and German. Among the works which he translated is The Aeneid. *He took part in the Cretan Rebellion of 1896, fought in the Balkan Wars of 1912 and died fighting, a Garibaldian officer, on Nov. 28, 1912. His works have been edited in one volume under the title* Works of Lorenzo Mavilis.

LETHE

Lucky are the dead who forget
life's bitterness. When the sun
goes down and clouds follow,
do not weep however you grieve.

At that hour, souls thirst and go
to oblivion's icy fountain;
but the water will blacken like slime,
if a tear falls from those they love.

And if they drink cloudy water they recall
crossing asphodel prairies and old pains
that lie dormant within them.

If you must weep at twilight,
let your eyes lament the living;
they long to but know not how to forget.

LORENZO MAVILIS

OLIVE TREE

In your hollow, hoary olive tree,
nests a bee-hive, bending with a fillet
of green still wound about you
as if to adorn you like a corpse.

And each little bird chirping
in love's giddiness starts
an amorous chase on your bough
on your boughs that will never bud again.

Oh how the beauties of lively youth
will sweeten you in death
with the magic sounds they make,

multiplying in you like memories;
ah, if other souls could die like this,
sisters of your soul.

IN SILENCE

Love flows like a river, and the greater its flow
the more it increases and in its sweet current
gleams the heavenly lie of happiness.
Love's course seems unending.

But before it, unexpected,
a bitter sea of pain spreads
full of tears and blood,
draining all, drenching all.

Mother dear, the leaves have withered
and winter presses close; I look
into your eyes and shudder with terror.

And your tranquil sick gaze
is startled as if asking:
"Will we enjoy another spring as before?"

SWEET DEATH

Sick one, see the day dies radiant—
rose portent of Death.
Drink deep of this serenity
that fate presents with open arms.

And in yonder temple gleaming white
the harmonies of a Pindaric ode
massing suddenly within the holy wind,
seem to stand like marble columns.

Enter, rest and sleep will cure you;
you will dream of beauty's being,
soothing with her ancient song

the harassed remnants of your heart.
"Those the gods love, perish young.
Awake not—I am lovely Death."

NOBLE PARENTAGE

(In Ancient Greece, the presence of women at the Olympic Games was not allowed.)

"My lady of Rhodes, how did you gain entrance?
An ancient custom denies entrance to women."
"I have a nephew, Eucleus, three brothers,
a son, a father—Olympian victors.

"You must let me enter, Judges.
I will glow with pride at the beautiful bodies
competing for the wild olive branch
of Hercules. Wondrous souls of men.

"I am not like other ladies;
through centuries my family will be famed
for their unfading claims to manliness.

"They are honored in letters of gold
on a gleaming slab of marble
by a golden hymn of the immortal Pindar."

C. P. CAVAFY

1868-1933. Born in Alexandria where his parents had migrated from Constantinople in 1840. The son of a wealthy merchant, he was educated in England. He returned to Alexandria upon the death of his father; worked as a civil servant for the Egyptian government. He was attracted to history, especially the period of Alexander the Great. He wrote his first poems in the purist. Cavafy had all his poems printed on loose leaf sheets which he distributed among his friends. He visited Athens only twice: once in 1904; and once just before his death for an operation on his throat. His language is demotic but it contains puristic idiosyncracies which he used deliberately to fit the mold of his themes. Cavafy died in Alexandria in 1933.

AWAITING THE BARBARIANS

"Why are we waiting, assembled in the public square?
    The barbarians enter the city today.
Why is the senate taking no action?
Why do the Senators sit and pass no laws?
    The barbarians enter the city today.
    What need for the Senators to legislate?
    When the barbarians come, they will make the laws.

"Why did our emperor wake up so early,
and sits at the principal gate of the city,
on the throne, so solemn, wearing his crown?
    The barbarians enter the city today.
    The emperor waits to receive
    their chief. He even prepared
    to hand him a scroll. Therein
    he heaped on him titles and honors.

"Why have our two consuls and the praetors come out
today in their purple, their embroidered togas?
Why did they wear amethyst studded bracelets
and rings with brilliant glittering emeralds?
Why did they carry costly canes today,
superbly carved with silver and with gold?
> The barbarians enter the city today.
> Such things dazzle the eyes of barbarians.

"Why do the eloquent speakers abstain
from making their speeches, from having their say?
> The barbarians enter the city today;
> they become bored with rhetorical speeches.

"Wherefore the tumult and sudden confusion?
(How long and serious the faces are now!)
Why are the streets and the squares clearing quickly,
and all return so pensive to their homes?
> Because night has come but not the barbarians.
> Some messengers returned from the border,
> they say barbarians no longer exist.

Now what shall we do without any barbarians?
Those people provided some sort of solution.

THE CITY

You said, "I will go to another land, to another sea.
Another city will be found better than this.
Each effort of mine is foredoomed to failure
and my heart is like a corpse—buried.
How long will my mind remain in this wasteland?
Wherever I turn my eyes, wherever I may look,

the black ruins of my life confront me here,
where for so many years I lived, consuming, despoiling.

You will find no new lands, no new seas.
The city will follow you. You will roam
the same streets. You will age in the same communities;
and you will grow white in these same houses.
All roads will lead you to this city. Do not hope to go else-
There is no ship for you, no street.　　　　　　　　　[where.
When you wasted your life here,
in this small corner, you ruined it for the whole world.

WALLS

Without thought, without remorse, without shame,
they built thick and high walls around me.

and now I sit despairing here.
I think of nothing else: this fate gnaws at my mind;

for I had many things to do outside.
Ah! Why didn't I see them as they built the walls.

But I never heard the noise of the builders.
Imperceptibly they shut me out of the world.

TROJANS

Our efforts are those of the ill-fated;
our efforts are like those of Trojans.
We succeed a little; we feel
somewhat relieved; we begin
to have courage and hope.

But something always appears to block us.
Achilles emerges in a trench
and with threatening cries dismays us.

Our efforts are like those of Trojans.
We think that with decision and daring
we will change the downdrag of fate,
and we stand armed for strife.

But when the great moment of crisis arrives,
decision and daring vanish;
our soul is troubled, numb;
and we run all around the walls
seeking a refuge in flight.

But our downfall is certain. Up there,
on the walls, the dirge has already begun,
they mourn the traditions and attitudes of our days.
Priam and Hecuba weep bitterly for us.

SATRAPY

What a pity, when you are made
for fine and important deeds
that always this unjust fate of yours
denies you encouragement and success;
base customs hinder you,
and pettiness, indifference.
And how dreadful the day when you yield,
(the day when you surrender and yield),
and you leave on foot for Sousa,
and you go to the King Artaxerxes,
who graciously admits you to his court
and he offers you satrapies and such.

and you accept in despair
these things you do not want,
while your soul yearns for other things and weeps
for the praise of the people and Sophists,
the hard-won, unbribed applause!
The agora, the theatre and the laurels.
Can Artaxerxes give these things to you?
Where will you find these things in a satrapy?
And bereft of these things, what life can you live?

ITHACA

When you start your voyage to Ithaca,
hope that the journey is long,
full of adventure, full of experience.
Do not fear irate Poseidon,
the Lestrigonians or the Cyclops.
You'll never meet such on your path,
if your mind is filled with lofty thoughts,
if fine emotions touch your body and soul.
You'll never meet the Lestrigonians,
the Cyclops, tumultuous Poseidon,
if you do not carry them in your heart,
if your mind does not erect them before you.

Hope that the voyage is long,
that the summer mornings are many,
that you enter ports first seen
with abounding pleasure and joy;
stop at Phoenician emporia,
and buy there wares of beauty,
corals, mother of pearl, amber and ebony too,
a medley of exotic perfumes,

buy as many exotic perfumes as you can;
visit hosts of Egyptian cities,
to learn and learn from the sages.
Keep Ithaca always fixed in your mind,
your goal is to arrive there.
But do not hurry the voyage at all;
let it rather last for many years;
and anchor the isle when already old,
enriched by all you garnered on the way.
Expect no rich returns from Ithaca.
Ithaca gave you the wondrous voyage.
Without her you never would have embarked.
But she has nothing more to give you now.

If you find her poor, Ithaca has not defrauded you.
You are become so wise from all your wandering,
you know by now what Ithacas mean.

IONIAN SONG

Because we broke their statues,
because we drove them from their temples,
this is why the gods have never died at all.
O Ionian land, they love you still.
It is you their spirits still cherish.
When the August morning dawns on you,
the vigor of their being passes through your air;
and at times, a figure of divine youth,
misty, in quiet passage,
traverses your hills.

GOD FORSAKES ANTHONY

When suddenly at midnight
the invisible troupe is heard passing
with glorious music and with song—
do not mourn in vain your waning fortune
your ventures that failed, your planned career
that has come to be an empty dream.
Be bold, as if for this you had been long prepared,
and for the last time, greet the Alexandria that is leaving.
Above all, do not be deluded or say it was
a dream and that your ears deceived you;
do not stoop to such empty hopes.
Be bold, as if for this you had been long prepared,
as it befits a man who merited a city such as this.
Approach the window with firm step
and listen with emotion, but not
with the pleas and plaints of the coward,
as a last pleasure, to the sounds,
the glorious instruments of the mysterious troupe,
and give her final greeting, the Alexandria you are losing.

RETURN

Return to me often and possess me,
beloved state, return and possess me—
when awareness in the body wakens,
and old desire again runs through the veins;
when the lips and the skin remember,
and the hands feel as if they touch once more.

Return to me often; possess me at night,
when the lips and the skin remember.

VERY SELDOM

He is an old man. Stooped and tired,
maimed by the years and by abuses too,
walking slowly, he steps across the road.
Yet as he enters his door to hide
the wretchedness of his old age, he muses
on the share he yet has of youth.

Now growing boys and girls recite his verses.
Through their lively eyes his fancies pass.
Their vigorous, sensuous minds,
their chiseled firm flesh
are stirred by his expression of beauty.

MANUEL KOMNINOS

The King Kyr Manuel Komninos
one melancholy September day
felt that death was near. The astrologers
(the bought ones) of the court babbled
that life had many years in store for him.
But while they said these very things,
an old hallowed custom came to his mind,
and from the cells of the monks he bade
them bring the gown of a monk,
and he wore it, and rejoiced that he presented
the modest aspect of a priest or a monk.

All are lucky who believe,
and like the King Kyr Manuel end their days,
clothed in their faith, most modestly.

FOR AMMONIS WHO DIED AT 29 in 610.

Raphael, they ask for some verses from you,
an epitaph for the poet Ammonis.
Something with taste and polish.
You are just the man to write
of Ammonis, the poet, who was ours.

Of course, you will speak of his work
but tell about his beauty too—
his delicate beauty that we loved.

Your Greek is lovely and musical always.
But now we have need of your utmost in skill.
Translate our love and sorrow to a foreign tongue.
Pour your Egyptian heart into a foreign tongue.

Raphael, you should write your verses so
that they will show, you understand, the flavor of our ways—
so that the rhythm and each phrase reveals
an Alexandrian is writing for an Alexandrian.

MORNING SEA

Let me stop here. Let me, too, see nature awhile,
morning sea and cloudless sky,
violet light and yellow sands;
all shining beautiful and large.

Let me stop here. Let me pretend I see these things
(Truly I saw them a moment when I first stopped)
and not that these too are my phantasies,
my memories, phantoms of pleasure.

SINCE NINE O'CLOCK

Half past twelve. The time has passed quickly
since nine when I lit the lamp
and sat down here. I sat without reading,
or speaking. To whom could I speak
all alone in this house?

Since nine when I lit the lamp,
the image of my young body
appeared and found and reminded me
of closed perfumed rooms,
and past pleasure—what daring pleasure!
It also brought before my eyes
streets that are now unrecognizable,
places full of movement that is ended,
and theatres and taverns that once were.

The image of my young body also
appeared and brought sad memories:
family mournings, separations,
thoughts of my dear ones, thoughts
of the dead, so slightly esteemed.

Half past twelve. How the time has passed!
Half past twelve. How the years have passed!

BODY REMEMBER

Body, remember not only how much you were loved,
not only the beds whereon you lay,
but also the desires that
glowed candidly in the eyes for you,

and trembled in the voice—a desire that
some chance obstacle left unfulfilled.
Now that all this belongs to the past,
it almost seems as if you had surrendered
to this desire—remember how it glowed,
in the eyes that regarded you,
how it trembled in the voice for you, remember, body.

OF THE SHIP

Of course this little pencil sketch
resembles him . . .
Quickly drawn, on the deck of the ship,
one enchanting afternoon,
the Ionian Sea all around us.

There is a likeness. But I remember him
as handsomer. He had rare sensitivity
and this gave added life to his expression.
He seems to me to have been handsomer
now that my soul evokes him from the long ago.

The long ago. How remote are all these things—
the sketch, the ship and the afternoon.

ONE OF THE JEWS (50 A.D.)

Painter and poet, runner and disk-thrower,
Janthis Antonios, handsome as Endymion,
from a family of people of the synagogue.

"My proudest days are those
when I have done with philosophic study,
when I abandon the beautiful, hard Hellenism
with its sovereign absorption
in perfectly shaped, perishable white limbs;
and I become the one I always yearned to be:
One of the Jews, the son of the holy Jews."
His declaration was very ardent. "Always
to be one of the Jews, the holy Jews."

But he did not stay such a man at all;
the hedonism and the arts of Alexandria
kept him a devoted disciple.

KOSTAS KRYSTALLIS

1868-1894. Born in Epirus. He was exiled by the Turks upon the appearance of his first volume of verse: Shadows of Hell. *He was influenced by the demotic songs of Valaoritis.* Works *(1891),* Poems of the Field, Songs of the Village and the Sheep-Fold *(1893),* Prose-Writing *(1894). He died of tuberculosis at Arta on April 22, 1894. His Complete Works appeared in 1912 and were re-edited in 1914. Palamas wrote a critical essay on* The Works of Krystallis *(1894). Michael Rodas wrote* The Life and Work of Kostas Krystallis.

I WOULD LOVE TO BE A SHEPHERD

I would love to be a shepherd or a shepherd's helper,
go and live in the sheep-fold, the desert, the woods,
have a flock of sheep, a flock of goats,
many sheep-dogs, have pastures too,
a fence of twigs, a sheepfold of holly,
a cave of oak on a high peak,
fun with the little shepherdess at milking time,
a flute to play on till the fields re-echo,
a pretty girl, my wedded bride,
to help me move the flock to pasture and gather them in.
Ah! to rest in the shadows at sunset
in the greenness of the ravine, to lie down with her,
to have her kiss me, to sleep on her cool breasts.

TO THE IMPERIAL EAGLE

My golden eagle, from a small, unnoticed fledgling
in time, you gain size, endurance, grace.

You spread your wings wide, tense your claws,
fly among the clouds, soar through the mountains,
nest in crevices, often discourse with the stars,
become enamoured of thunder, leap and play
with wild thunder-bolts and the birds of the field
and mountain robins name you king.

Thus a small desire in my breast was born,
and from an unseen, featherless fledgling, my golden eagle,
it grew, took on wings, body and claws,
and it drains my heart, it tears my soul;
now my longing is an eagle, a spectre, a dragon,
nesting deep in my wasted body,
secretly gnawing my vitals, grazing in secret on my youth.

I am weary of walking fields in sun and gale.
I wish to climb the heights; I wish to anchor, my eagle,
in my old home, my first nest.
I wish to anchor on the mountains, I want to live with you.
I wish the wild boar, the bear, the stag,
to be my close, daily companions.
Each evening, each dawn, I want the cold air
to come out of the gorge, like a mother, a sister,
to caress my hair and my open breast.

I wish the spring, the ravine, my old sweet loves,
to heal me with their immortal waters.
I wish the warbling birds of the gorge
to lull me to sleep in the evening, wake me at dawn.
I wish as bed and cover
branches in the summer, snow in the winter,
forked fires, twigs of wild shrubs,
I wish to spread heaps of them and lie down
hearing the echo of the rain and sleeping sweetly.

O eagle, I wish to chew acorns from a gentle oak,
I wish to swallow deer cheese and wild goat's milk,
I wish to hear pines and beeches shrieking about me,
I wish to walk cliffs, chasms, high boulders,
I wish to see waterfalls right and left,
I wish to hear you filing your claws on the rocks,
to hear your raucous cry, to see your shadow. I want
but I have no eagle's wings, I am wingless,
and I suffer, I ache, and I waste away night and day.
O eagle, swoop down a little I beg,
lend me your wings and carry me with you
up to the mountains. The fields will devour me.

THE VINTAGE

When the creeping vine blooms and spreads her tendrils
towards the reeds, the bushes, the branches of pine,
the river beds, the rocky cliff;
the winds, field and mountains—all creation—
is filled with the fragrance of her breath.
As a dense black swarm of bees pours out
of rocks and lilies, deserts and gardens,
to feed on the flowers, inhale their perfume,
buzzing and droning in delight,
so the village girls pour out of their homes,
disperse to fields and mountains, run where there are vines,
with wicker baskets, sickles, singing,
with gladness when the vintage starts.

Desert places are full of movement, the vines rustle.
Bodies of girls seem to sprout from each jutting rock,
from sorrel creeping on the grass,
the green vines reach out with the heavy grapes,

black, gold and yellow, here forming black bunches, here
under the first rays of the sun-heat rising,   [glistening,
like black eyes or like thick clusters of pearls.
The haughty stems gleam too
and the vine arbors stretch to the broad beds
and with their dense foliage and thick shade
they refresh the sweating laborers who take breath—
the laborers gathering grapes daily, spreading them out,
the laborers longing for the sun to go down,
for the mountain slopes to shade, the fields to cool.

See the sun has already set, gone down,
see the mountain slopes are shaded, the field is cooler,
the sun completely gone. The mountains darken,
the clear waters deepen, and overhead the stars come out.
The laborers breathe deeply and cease their work
and where you see the vine branches and fence of twigs,
they weave a hut; they sit around their frugal meal
and a dim oil-lamp sheds light on their simple supper.
Then in each vineyard, each slope, each vine,
bright fires are lit in the dark expanse.
Round and round the fires, the girls start a dance;
old and young stretch out on the ground and one of them
accompanies the dance with a soft song,
and a soft, soft beat of a mandolin,
till the stars of the sky mark the midnight,
then the dances break, the laborers disperse;
they spread branches for beds and wearied they lie down,
and here and there, where the scattered fires die,
the sleepless night bird lulls them sweetly to sleep
till the burst of the morning star when they will awaken again,
again to start their work at the prized vintage.

THE EMBROIDERY ON THE KERCHIEF

At the edge of the shore sits a yellow-haired girl,
embroidering in gold a fine white kerchief,
a kerchief for the groom, her wedding gift.
She embroiders the sea with all its islands,
the sky with all its shimmering stars,
the earth with its many beautiful flowers.
She also embroiders a steep, wide mountain;
the dawn breaks gently on its crest,
and the ribbon of sky is dyed rose-white.
Clear silvery waters come pouring down
to furrow the broad and open slopes.
She embroiders in green silk thread the ravines,
the deep, shaded thickets of thousands of years.
Flocks like white groups at the foot of the hill
and shepherds appear; in the lovely embroidery
you seem to hear flutes, and singing,
hoarse bleatings and cow-bell tunes.

At the mountain's base she sets an azure lake
with golden reeds. A fisherman at the edge
holding a dragnet prepares the bait.
All around she embroiders with emerald thread
a very wide field, in the center of the field
she draws a quiet, serpentine river,
with plane trees, myrtles, laurels,
nightingales and nests. In the beauteous design
you seem to hear the murmuring water,
to smell the bay and the myrtle leaves,
to hear the song of nightingales,
to feel the gentle rustle of the foliage.
At the river bank she draws a deer
bending to drink the icy waters.
Suddenly an arrow wounds his side;

he whirls, looks at the wound in pain;
struggles to free himself but wretched cannot.
He seems to be seeking help
from the sky, from the trees all about.
Around the valley
she embroiders here tiny villages, there fields,
golden grain with stacks and threshing floors,
green vines with yellow grapes
yellow like coins, and beautiful little girls
entering with woven baskets, gathering grapes.
She embroiders a lavish village wedding—
the bride, the groom, the banners of the nuptial train.
Elsewhere she embroiders dragons, ogres,
Nereids and a sparkling sapphire sea.
At the edge of the sea she embroiders herself
in all her loveliness and youth,
wealth and position, holding in white hands
the kerchief, her exquisite embroidery,
for the groom, her wedding gift.
She embroiders slowly and never stops her song:
"Dear richly-colored, gold-embroidered kerchief,
who may he be, the young man who receives you?
What young man will he be, Oh precious kerchief,
who will receive you with a ring as wedding gift?
Who will the young man be who with a kiss,
burning and sweet, as he holds my white hand,
will lead me to the virgin bed a bride?
Who will he be? Tell me, you little trees
and you dear birds, whisper soft to me,
you beautiful shore and dear azure sky!
You, my winged, crystal thoughts!
Can you not say who he may be, show him to me,
bring him to me in secret one fine evening,
like a golden dream, sweetly to my embrace?"

KOSTES HATZOPOULOS

> *1869-1920. Born in Agrinion. Pseudonym of Petros Vasilikos. He studied law but devoted himself exclusively to literature. He lived in Germany for many years, and translated Goethe's* Faust. *He founded the review* Art *in Athens (1898-99).* Poetic works: The Songs of Solitude, Elegies and Idylls, Simple Ways, Evening Noises. *Prose works:* Tasso, Autumn, The Book of the Younger Brother.

LET THE BOAT GO . . .

Let the boat go where it will on the wave,
let the breeze steer rudder and sail.
Spread the wings wide, the earth has no end;
unknown shores are always beautiful.
Life is a dew-drop, a wave, let the breeze
carry the boat where it will, where it knows.

Let prairie scenes turn to forests and rocks,
let towers, the smoke of the hut pass before you.
Whether nature spreads a laughing idyll before you,
or heaven hangs out its thunder or storms,
do not think you can hold the sail fast to the course—
you will anchor with the wave, wherever it wills.

Do you know in your heart what you want and are seeking?
Have you ever caught what you have hunted?
Do you not reap ill for the good that you sow?
Do you not stumble even phrasing a query?
Is yours the cunning, is yours the effort
that has led you astray, that has cheated you?

Then let the wave break where it will,
let dizziness lead your heart blindly,
and though clouds may gather, though winds may moan,
the sun on some shore must be smiling,
and if bitter tears spray your heart,
know that somewhere a hidden joy awaits.

MILTIADES MALAKASSIS

> 1870-1943. Born in Missolonghi. He wrote poems at an early age, and later published Hours, Destinies, Asphodels. *He was director of the Library of the Greek Parliament. On Jan. 27, 1943 he died, having suffered privations during the Nazi occupation.*

BATTARIAS

> "A Saturday night,
> a Sunday morning!" . . .

Young Boukouvala and Klys, Tsangarakis' son,
and Brana's son, Nikos,
sometimes of a Saturday night, drowned their sorrows in drinking at Vlaho's. [secret,

And since the three were well-bred, at the height of the fun,
they'd send for violins,
and soon they'd spy Peter Katsaros,
and behind him Thanasy Battaria.

And together with the lute player, the fiddler,
and the flutist,
they'd start for the farmstead of Kosta Kaliantery,
who was sure to be there.

And Kosta, cat-napping, always with his apron on,
would jump to his feet,
and haul the table down toward the waterside,
in the light of the broad sea-lake.

And when it was set and arranged, and the instruments
had been tuned, softly

the folk songs would begin, the Oriental tunes
that are as kindling on the hearth.

Then as they sat at the table and you lifted your voice,
O great Battaria!
with the third glass of wine, birds of Paradise
awakened on the boughs.

Little by little, O wonder, as you reached the heart of the
gallant deeds and desires,   [song,
you exalted both love and the mountaineer
to the stars, to the moon, to the very gods.

From those heights where no one can reach,
where even breath itself is caught,
playing merrily, your skylark's voice
glided the scale down to base.

And as often happened, the joy of summer
crowned such pleasures,
the world outdoors, waters and fields wafting fragrance,
everything growing mightily,

even the least forward stepped out
to hear and see;
not a twenty-year old who did not come outdoors, nor young
who did not step into the road.   [widow

Even the very young, unable to climb over
enclosures and courtyards
pricked up their small snail-like ears to hear,
their eyes to dart arrows.

And the songs—breezes refreshing yet burning—
O woeful passion!
Sometimes they brought flames, sometimes the fountain's
spray to the heart's foliage.

But where the voice moves the heart like an ocean,
the giddy mind strays
not knowing where, with lost wings
in fog and oceans of desire.

As the night paled and the joyous dawn
beamed on their faces,
Battarias stopped all at once and threw the bow
with its last sobbing note into the waters.

And standing up, beckoning to the others to get ready,
and bending to his three
guests, newly grown up, whose heads were full of
the night's smoking,

the sober one told them that it was not proper,
in the morning and on Sunday,
to see boys who were properly reared,
mixed up with violins and wine.

And while he told them these things, the uptown marketers,
as if in a daze,
took the shore road; the downtown marketers
took the narrow lanes.

In broad daylight, the golden bells
began to ring;
the girls went in to sleep, and the mothers
went in to dress and go to church . . .

SPRING STORM

Heavy, broad,
large and widely scattered,

the drops of rain
come down!
A mute weeping, but what a clamor!
How you re-echo
within sad hearts!
You are like the broken strokes of the bow.
How cruel are old wounds,
and the despairs
of wretched
waiting! . . .
See
the March sun,
hard as the hail,
hard as the stars.
Oh woe! It lives
among the other things
of the storm.
The drop of water
also has a life of its own
—as now it trickles—
into the porce-
lain
flowerpot.
This evening,
this evening
my whole life is linked
to all the rustling, the leaf-shedding.
The rain beats down, it writhes,
and it is brother to my pain.
This evening the veiled sun
shines white,
it sinks
without fire
as does my lost soul

into our net, O rain!
and into your wasteland
oh hail . . .

THE FOREST

The forest you dreaded
to walk through,
now you may forget,
evening passerby.

Sweatless wood-cutters
looted it one morning;
now there are only roads,
evening passerby.

You will hear no more
the heavy sigh
that touched your heart
and shook your knees.

The birds of the night
have carried it away on their wide
terrified wings
and made it their cry.

And something hoarsely crying
in a human voice—
it too has become still
in the hush of the place.

And the menacing gleam
of the bare blood-stained knife
you saw held in a hand
has gone.

MILTIADES MALAKASSIS

The soft singing
that lured you, passerby,
to a haunted palace,
with never a hope of dawn,

see they carried it away.
A last shudder—
the dead leaves
left on the ground.

And the harp with its melody
that made you sweetly drunk,
but that secretly plucked
the music of death,

is lost, not to be heard again
on seas and mountains,
with the untouched
girl who played it.

The forest you dreaded
to walk through,
you may forget forever,
evening passerby.

The savage trees you saw
are coffins now
scattered over the land,
evening passerby.

TAKIS PLUMIS

When I was a child, my eldest cousin
used to take me with him to the fairs

where he was above all others
first in looks and spirits.

How handsome! I remember how he sparkled
mounted on his steed, flaunting
a cherry-coloured, gold-embroidered jacket
and spangles of Venetian florins.

He wore the scimitar of Captain Pasha,
and the knife of Botsari,
and right and left across the saddle
hung two pistols from the treasury of Ali.

He wore an even-hemmed short fustanella,
stockings and pom-pom shoes
ordered and delivered from Janina,
silver hooks from Prevesa.

Thus bedecked with the long musket
across his shoulder, mane and reins
in his hands, he dazzled the road
catapulting out of the broad gate!

And I, a short distance behind him,
a-glitter on my fleet colt,
tried hard as I could to overtake him,
and I felt I had wings, a small weightless body.

And as we raced, I remember his curly hair
clustered about his Tunisian fez,
gleaming like a little cloud
of blazing hay.

And as he grew hotter still in the race,
tempestuous, enveloped with light,
he seemed to be sheathed in gold as he rode,
the image of Saint George, only a little shorter.

Oh the gallants of our Missolonghi—
the sun of the brief dawn of my life!
Now that I count back, Takis Plumis
is thirty-three years in the earth . . .

YIANNIS GRIPARIS

1872-1942. Born on the island of Syphinos, and studied in Constantinople. Later he completed his studies at the University of Athens. He published Scarabes; Terra Cotta (1920). *He translated Aeschylus, Sophocles, Euripides and Plato. Griparis was Inspector General of Public Education. He died on March 10, 1942. Other works:* Elegies, Intermedia, The Ivy, After Rain.

MOUNT RHODOPE

The seven-fold star of the Pleiades hangs low in the sky,
Rhodope, awake! The dawn shakes off the frozen dew,
the drowsiness of sleep; awake for the sweet, joyous dawn
is still pale as dull torquoise.

The red-gold sun will bring you many roses,
old as his love, fresher than the hail;
now he comes forth and kissing your brow,
with amorous hands sets there his dewy wreaths.

Night still reigns in the ravines, the curly
forests, the valleys see not a single sunbeam,
and the Strymon flows, dragging low at her feet.

But Rhodope, bathed in light, pillars her peak
in the highest heaven, and over her, like a dew-drop
on rose-leaves, the last star of morning gleams.

VESTAL VIRGINS

Deep mute midnight, skies pitch-black
over the slumbering city.

YIANNIS GRIPARIS

Suddenly the Spirit of Evil shrieks a piercing shriek,
a voice of dread—and all leap up perturbed.

"The everlasting fire is out!" and all rush
blindly into the night to arrive in time
not with the hope that the calamity is false
but that their eyes might see and be indulged.

It seemed as if the dead had left their cobwebby tombs
in time for the final judgment,
and although the unwary writhe in an evil nightmare,
they tremble lest someone awaken them.

Despairing, as if with one choking sob,
they go forth to the Temple of Vesta,
and before the bronze gate, wide-open
countless eyes look on as one.

This they see: dressed in the futile dignity
of their noted ancient virtue,
kneeling before the betrayed altar,
the modest Vestal Virgins, now damned.

Their sin was a hesitating, indolent
carelessness, like that of my own youth!
But the Holy Flame, since it is out, can never be relit
by human kindling or fire-giver.

And no matter how much they pull at their hair
with humility and contrition,
all is vain! Now in the cool cinders and ashes
no trace of spark or hope is left.

And the fall of the City is fated unless
before the new sun rises heaven performs
a miracle and in the deep of night,
forbearing, sends down its lightning.

And if it is to strike them, let it strike!
As the heavens demand justice, so the Virgins demand it.
See them, with their hands uplifted,
their souls in their eyes calling upon it.

.   .   .   .

Did this miracle really happen? You tell me; then I'll tell you,
O irresolute, unjust mind of youth,
like my own, extinguished without purpose,
but still alive, seething with its purpose!

REVEILLE FOR THE DEAD

The stars flicker and there is little left of night;
under a pale sick light the valleys brighten,
and all around, wherever your eye turns,
it sees bodies blackening strewn here and there.

Death mingles friends and foes at one feast
where uninvited beasts roam hungrily;
fortunate the man who is saved, the man who escaped,
those torn by the bullet are torn again by the crows.

Suddenly the wounded bugler leaps to his feet
the bugle blows in a shrill, lacerating voice
rending no ears—but its own brass.

But none of the dead awaken at reveille,
only flocks of crows fly away as if they are
the souls of the slain going to heaven.

YIANNIS GRIPARIS

COMRADES IN DEATH

The curse of the father
girdled their threefold loins.
They took the first road
they met before them.
Somber, dismal rebels against God
take whatever road they meet.

The Adversary summoned them
at harvesting time.
The ripe grain was blanched
on the plentiful earth,
and the scythe on the whetstone
was like the grinding of teeth.

On sides and on slopes
where no plow can approach,
swarms of souls like an ant-hill
blacken the space;
one would think even the very roads
moved with the somber walkers.

At the edge of the precipice,
at the edge of the abyss,
listen, foe calls to foe.
"Wait for me, I'll go with you!"
"Go on, wherever you go,
I'll find the black tracks of your feet."

Their hesitating thought wavers
between the yes and the no,
whether to take the right or left
of the forked crossroads;
they stop and then with a new rush
they start on their way once more . . .

It is no longer daybreak,
it is not yet evening,
but soon they will arrive
their hearts in their mouths.
As you know all roads lead to
Rome of the Seven Hills.

PETROS VLASTOS

1879-1941. Born in Calcutta. Pseudonym for Ermonas. He studied law in Athens and lived in England. He is the author of: Argo, At the Shade of the Fig Tree, *and* Grammar of the Demotic Language.

TO MY MOTHER

My mother was embroidering, bent, by the window.
Outdoors the last raindrops were falling on the downy fields
and the freshly bathed hedges. The eyes of spring
laughed and cried, openly, and girlish tears

rolled sweet and slow on the earth's green.
Near our garden, a silver breasted poplar
drew its leaves close to itself, and the raindrops,
sliding step by step on the leaves, came down.

And they made music softly. Hanging dim and low,
the setting sun looked back and with the flash of its ray
lit tremulous, water-shimmering sparks on the boughs.

A blessed calm had spread around
and my mother laid her embroidery aside and rose
to listen to the song of the slow, dewy life.

THE VILLAGE OF LOVE

Shadows cover the village lanes
and darken the row of door-sills.
Farm animals fill the courtyards; at the fountain
girls appear white, their earthenware jars on the ground.

Over the enclosure, the sparse leaves of the fig tree
stand diaphanous gold and the vine leaves
redden on the branches. The fragrance of the new wine
pours into the air from wine skins and wine presses.

Somewhere you smell freshly baked bread. The goat
on the pebbly stone ledge sits chewing the cud, glancing
[obliquely
on the threshing floor and in the valleys, already harvested

the amber wheat is thickly stacked
and the lost soul recalls an old tune
for in a village like this nested the house of his love.

LAMBROS PORPHYRAS

1879-1933. Born in Chios but lived most of his life in Piraeus. Pseudonym of Demetrios Sypsomos. He studied law at the University of Athens. He went to France, England, Italy. He published: Shadows *(1920, 1924);* Musical Voices. *The French government and the Academy of Athens awarded him the highest poetry prizes. Several articles about his work have been published in* Nea Estia.

LACRIMAE RERUM

Poor girl! Our little home is haunted
by your sad loveliness!
On the walls, the mirror, the icons,
something of your beauty remains.

Something like musk-fragrance spreads
and floods the humble little home.
Something like a ghost, hazy, intangible,
lightly touches wherever it passes.

Outdoors, a heavy monotonous downpour
lashes our roof. Within, altogether,
the objects that your hands made holy
start a-weeping . . . a-weeping . . .

And in the corner, Lethe's fine companion,
the old clock loved by us,
the singer of passing time, is weeping too.
Evenly, awesomely, it ticks out the dirge . . .

THE LAST FAIRY-TALE

They followed the path all the way,
princesses and fairies,
kings from foreign lands,
and horsemen riding.

Round my grandma's bed,
between two pallid torches,
they passed and like minstrels
they sang to her—who knows what song.

No one for love of my grandma
killed dragon or ogre,
to bring her immortal water.

My mother was kneeling
but overhead, once upon a time—
the Archangel beat his wings.

THE TRIP

The sun-glad day is a wondrous dream. Annoula and I,
a few of my old comrades with some girls,
stepped into a bright blue, tipsy little boat.
We stepped in for we are heading far, for the isle of Joy.

Not a trace of cloud or fog in the breeze;
beside us amorous breasts, white snowy necks,
light on gold hair, light on the sea, the horizon,
but who ever found the isle of Joy?

Ah! What matter if we go that far? What matter?
All my dear companions laugh, sorrowful life laughs,

we roll in space and Annoula sings with mad abandon:
"No matter how distant, the isle of Joy will appear."

EPIGRAM

Here at this solitary spring,
where the shadow of a beauty
wandered, untouched
in the nacreous deep,

I dedicate a wreath
of wild flowers
and hang it on the willow branch
for the little water-nymphs.

Sadly, I beg the reeds
to sing with the flutes
the unspoken tender words
that are long dead,

and the spring in the hollow
of the rock to pour
as into an urn,
her musical tears.

ZACHARIAS PAPONDONIOU

1872-1942. Born at Karpenissiou. He worked as a journalist and wrote a reader for children in the demotic, entitled High Mountains. *His* War Songs *was printed after the unsuccessful war of 1897. He published* Prose Rhythms *and* The Swallows. *He was director of the School of Fine Arts. He published his impressions of his journeys to Constantinople and Mount Athos in a book called* The Living Byzantium. *Another book of travel impressions is entitled* The White Island of Tinos. Divine Gifts *appeared in 1931.*

THE PRAYER OF THE HUMBLE

Lord, since the night has come, I say my prayer to Thee.
I have harmed no soul in the world but my own.
They wounded me who were dear to me.
I endured my own sorrows. You gave me those of strangers.

Joys shunned me. I no longer seek them.
I await the worst. To hope is sinful.
As good fortune I welcome the menace of night.
No one ever knocks at my door but the wind.

I have no fame. The deeds I have done are quiet ones.
I have listened to the sweet rain. I have watched the sun go
I have given children joy; fondled dogs a little.   [down.
I have greeted the plowmen returning at night.

Now I have nothing to strive for or call my own.
I await no reward. Such a hope is too bold.
Grant that I die and never live again.
I thank Thee for the mountains, the fields I have seen.

SERENADE AT THE WINDOW
OF THE WISE MAN

Wise man, the fourfold wise
lantern shedding light on you
says if only it were a moon
and you were only twenty.

If only your learning could
dispute with the breeze
about a forested hill,
a fresh morning start . . .

If only your thoughts were
songs for a syrto dance,
an armful of flowers,
a silly tale.

The thousand things you never knew
would have been clear as water,
if suffering, a stolen kiss
had been your teacher.

You have scorned life
much, a curse on it . . .
And now? It is fled
like a morning dream.

Lovely lips of your neighbors bloom,
carnations bloom in the flower pot—
and you read the stars
and the deep sky.

SAD SUNSETS

In the neighborhood slums
my mind turns to the lanes,
I think of the sad sunsets
of Sunday.

Within the red afterglow
the faded girl
without hope or speech
waters the mint.

No walker passes by;
she who stands on the balcony
wearing her new garnet dress
waits for no one.

An old woman sits like a Fate
in the light of a ruined door,
the shadow of a child lengthens . . .
A bell is heard afar.

In the cherry colored cloud
the sun will sink and hide.
The voice of the last peddler
is heard like a chant.

Everything is still.
The night is long in coming . . .
How heavy is my soul,
on Sunday afternoon.

MARIGO

Our servant girl Marigo
doesn't do anything right.
She forgets about our kitchen
and remembers the village.

Her little hands are here,
but her brain is down below.
She falls and breaks the dish,
Marigoula, Marigo!

She carries water on her shoulder,
but then she recalls:
"Who is rocking our baby?"
She spills half on the road.

"The white chicken, what is she doing?
The pig, has it grown strong?
Grandpa, I hope he doesn't die . . ."
Marigoula, Marigo!

"The goose must have goslings;
they must be yellow, gray;
we'll be harvesting this month;
Granny must have surely missed me."

"What have you in your eyes, cloud?
Why are you sobbing so?"
Another dish in smithereens,
Marigoula, Marigo!

Take your white Sunday dress
and the aprons I bought you to wear.
To your village, to your village,
Marigoula, Marigo!

THE OLD SHEPHERD

I have lived so many years;
I have grown white and old
on the high mountains
grazing the sheep!

I have stood on summits
and walked in the night,
and in aged, hoary trees,
I have seen fairies many times.

I swooped like a blackbird
on towering cliffs.
I fell into ravines
sleeping lightly as a hare.

In my capote,
my clothes and my mattress,
wide awake or sound asleep,
dozing, I saw dreams.

I have climbed the eagle's eyrie
I have quarreled with the wolf,
I have kindled huge fires
on soaring summits.

I saw the star on the mountain
they call the morning star,
and in the clear night
I drank deep of starry sky.

I never hurt an ant,
I have angered no man.
I carried little lambs
like infants in my arms.

I have lived a lifetime
and God willed that I grow old,
and the heavy snow
has fallen on my head.

Come, my little sheep,
walk, my little lambs.
Let us go slowly, slowly;
night has overtaken us.

APOSTOLOS MELACHRINOS

1880—. Born at Vraila, Rumania. He lived in Constantinople, where he edited the magazine Life. *He wrote* Poetic Works, The Road Leads, *and* Magic Refrains. *He edited a collection of* Demotic Songs *and translated a great many of the ancient Greek tragedies into modern Greek. He lives in Athens and is editor of the magazine* The Cycle. *On his fortieth anniversary in the field of letters the poets of Greece honored Melachrinos by dedicating an entire issue of* The Cycle *to his work.*

PLAYING THE LYRE (from APOLLONIUS)

Once there lived in a land,
(come join the dance!)
in a faraway land, in a distant land,
a maid of high repute,
(you have driven me mad!)
a maid of high repute, most fair and a rich man's daughter.

Of all who went
(now you lead the dance!)
of all who went to see her, none returned,
for in an instant
(you have driven me mad!)
for in an instant they were struck down and took other roads!

The widow's only son,
(mind the dance well!)
the widow's only son returned one day,
but no one
(you have driven me mad!)
but no one learned what he had seen or heard.

APPOSTOLOS MELACHRINOS

Except that he sings,
(health to you, my gallants!)
except that he sings on the road, as if possessed
that he is wedded to her,
(you have driven me mad!)
that he is wedded to the fairest and is king of the world.

MAGIC REFRAINS (from VARIATIONS)

In the rustle of the twilight dream,
a rose-elegy tells a fairy-story.
New, unaccustomed rhythms
disturb the slow twilight.

Satyrs danced lewdly
on an ancient rich grass
while Pan the dreamer played the flute
at an Arethousian fountain.

Nymphs with disheveled hair
gathered western roses.
They mourned Hyacinthus
on fairy guitars.

In the rustle of the ancient grass
the green rhythm shuddered
and the sorcerer reigned
on Narcissan-like waters.

Solitary soul, abandon
the litany of flowers.
You leave in despair
for the uncertain road,

And you light the candle
before the Madonna of Sorrows.
In the rustle of the twilight dream
a rose-elegy tells a fairy story.

IT IS RAINING AGAIN

It is raining again!
On deserted back streets
the psalms you read at matins lament.
Your sweet-smelling little soul made fragrant
your body erect in worship.

It is raining again!
On the dull panes of the cell,
mystic icons weep
where suns painted with their blood
your incense-sprayed psalms.

It is raining again!
The weeping rain is like an echo
in your misty memory.
You would think it was nature's prayer
and your soul weeps for something it craves.

It is raining again!
Why do yearnings always say, *Remember?*
Their rainy psalms
have drenched your immaculate soul
and cannot endure in tears.

It is raining again!

NICHOLAS KARVOUNIS

1880-1946. Born in Ithaca. Studied in Rumania. He wrote for newspapers, and directed the magazines Politea *and* Estia. *In 1912 he joined the Garibaldians as a volunteer. He fought in every war from 1913 to 1946, when he died. His best known writing is a prose work entitled* The Greek Bulgarian War. *In World War II he was cultural director of the EAM and wrote many stirring war songs. He translated Walt Whitman into demotic Greek.*

THE SONG OF THE VANQUISHED

My soul is a lifeless Venice
in a dead, waveless sea.

Her dark, desolate palaces are mute, dismal,
with the heavy casements locked forever.
They press their cold shadows on the sleepy canals
that gondolas of joy, love gondolas
will furrow no more, never more.
Nor will soft strumming guitars stir
from their never waking sleep
deep echoes as of yore
under the arches of the sad bridges.

My soul is a lost Venice
in a dead, endless sea.

Beneath distant, nostalgic horizons
some forgotten evening, the sun rested
on its bed torpid and dying;
and dragging itself hoplessly in deep swelling waves;
in a torrent of golden hair,

her luminous quivering roses,
forever defoliate . . .
And the eternal night spread itself everywhere—
the moonless, starless, sterile night
that does not presage a bright new dawn.

My soul is a Venice fallen asleep,
in the cold deeps of a dreamless slumber.

A shadow resembling me wanders
in the silent breadth of the corridors
of the ducal palace
awaiting the governor Doge.
I think he will never return
for he cast his betrothal ring into the dead sea
and his heavy crown into the stagnant water
and he was lost in the mystery of the deepest crypts
the keys of which were swallowed by Lethe.

Far-off, on strange, distant horizons
the timid and frail hours stopped
folding their tireless wings
for in the dark they saw
the giant shadow of eternity towering before them
with the austere finger of command at the lips.
A sadness spreads over all—
nostalgic, like the wreath, that forgotten memento
of a fabulous first of May—
withered years ago on the balcony
of the locked dismal house
deserted even by the swallows, all in decay
awaiting a May that will never return.

My soul is a lost Venice
in a fathomless, dead unmoving sea.

Some hours of the darkness
nocturnal phantoms appear, mistily lit and diaphanous,
plainly steering a white ship.
What breeze is filling its sails
on the unwrinkled sea of death?
In the forepart of the prow in an open coffin
with lips tight sealed, in a strengthless stubbornness,
with eyes closed fast and with hands that clasp
to a cold breast a sword thenceforth useless,
the vanquished hunter of the dream sleeps heavily
and it is I . . . it is I . . .

Then in the highest tower of the ducal palace
the shadow resembling me appears
to assume the guise of the dead traveller
and he stretches out hopelessly his tired hands
in voiceless and heavy longing;
but he waits in vain. The mystic ship
sails slowly; the foam
on the prow does not roar, nor does
memory furrow the sea behind
and it blows out in the darkness and distance.

My soul is a lost Venice . . .

It is not fated that the bronze lions of night
shake the rich mane
with the moan of joy; silent forever
beneath their high domes the harmony of faith,
the indomitable pride of the towers
is extinguished in the eternal night.
A shadow resembling me wanders
condemned by fate, beneath the arches
of the bitter Bridge of Sighs,
waiting in vain for a storm or upheaval

to disturb the mute waters
or to pull down the desolate city to the deeps.

My soul is a lost Venice
that does not even wait for death.

SOTIRIS SKIPIS

1881–. Born in Athens. He studied literature in Greece and Paris. Poetic works include: Songs of the Orphan, Serenade of the Flowers, Silenti Dissolutio, The Great Breath, Juvenilia, Trophies in the Tempest, The Imperishable, The Apollonian Song, The Aeolian Harp, Flowers of Solitude, Midas of Azure, Colchides. *He translated into the demotic the* Works and Days *of Hesiod and some of the verse of J. Moreas. He is also the author of a prose work,* The Black Dog, *and editor of an anthology of contemporary lyric poetry.*

O SWEET ATHENS

Sweet Athens! I dream once more
of your winter, when the rain
starts of a sudden and walkers
scatter hurriedly from your streets.

Beneath the cornice of a shut store
I will find shelter
and I will remain alone for hours
to hear the sad downpour of song.

Ah, drops of rain! What faded echo of
dearly loved voices do you bring to me?
What faraway happiness that did not last?
What undying yearning?

Once I used to hear you from the window
Of my house, O Athenian rain!
But death sealed the door
and fate warped it forever.

YOU WILL REMEMBER ME

You will remember me when a misty ray
of a flickering light will shine on
your inner world; when lulled
by hopes of futile rising.

When you will cry out, Oh dearest,
as if in a nightmare: "Come back to me,
for night has come menacing, furious,
pressing on my poor heart."

And as always I will want to come; but
it will be late, and only in a vision.
somewhere you will discern me again,
then quickly I will melt in your blurred phantasy.

MYRTIOTISSA

1882–. *Pseudonym for Theoni Dracopoulou. Born in Constantinople. Myrtiotissa was an actress and later a professor of speech at the Conservatory of Athens. Poetic works:* Songs, Poems For Recitation *with a preface by Kostes Palamas,* A Children's Anthology of Best Greek Poems *in rhyme, prefaced by Kostes Palamas. The Gifts of Love (1932) won her the award from the Academy of Athens.* Cries *won her the National Poetry Prize. She translated a collection of poems by Comtesse de Noailles (1928).* Yellow Flames *(1946) contains a preface by Kostes Palamas. A number of her poems have been translated into French, English and German.*

WOMEN OF SULI

(During the Greek War of Independence of 1821, all the women of Suli leaped to their death with their children in their arms from the cliffs of Zalongo in Epirus, rather than surrender to the Turks.)

Ah! You who wakened in my child's soul
the first quiver of phantasy and wonder,
who first opened the deeps of my heart
for the sublime breath of poetry to enter!

Ah! You who wakened in me a vast pride,
what if my life is a starless night,
what if a wasteland, bitter and black, surround me,
if only a drop of your blood beats in my heart!

As a child, I leaned on my grandmother's knee
to hear of princesses most fair and mighty kings,

but always at the end, I remembered to ask about you,
"Tell me your story, Grandma, the true story."

And as she began, I saw you passing before me,
one by one, like high-breasted, beautiful princesses,
and singing still, you plunged into the dragon's cave
imbedded at the base of the cliff.

Then terrified I closed my eyes and always
the moan of your wild song would reach my ears,
weaving a living circle in my mind,
yawning mouths of an unseen monster.

But though my early years were full of you, your meaning
escaped me, for it was greater than my mind could grasp,
I loved you with a seven year old heart
I thought of you with timid, quivering love.

As my emotion deepened and thought matured,
once as I stood beneath the spreading red-gold light
diffused over Zalongo before the sun went down,
I saw a miraculous vision of your tragic dance!

And I saw you like young does ascending
with your children, a sheer and rugged peak,
the sun crowning the serpents of your hair,
rags covering your bodies teeming with life.

And you tossed down your children, and ah me, the infants
seemed to be playing a happy mad game;
at the foot of the cliff were piled roses and lilies
that shone like an April garden, softly.

And then of a sudden you started a frenzied celebration,
One by one, dropping into space, you left the dance,
and you wheeled in ever narrowing circles
and the wind flailed many colored rags and hair!

Abruptly my heart shook, a worshipping bell,
for you were left the last, alone on the peak,
and I quaked like a terrified mother . . .
but you were rigid and still, last woman of Suli!

Ah! When your scream had trailed away, your feet were in
when the tight-clenched fingers flew apart like birds,   [space,
and you saw about you only thorns and stones
in the frightful and infinite gloom enclosing you,

did horror not glide snake-like through your heart,
did doubt not face you for a moment
as you measured the yawning abyss before you,
did death not seem a foe worse than the Turk?

The others rested sweetly in the feathery arms of glory,
leaned down from the whirl of their sacred dance,
but you were awakened bitterly by silence
fixing its cold glance upon you.

Then, did your beloved country scenes not haunt you?
The rough path leading to the village?
Did you not feel your mother's trembling touch
under the pine shading your house, like a mighty guardian?

Did you not hear your dogs bay mournfully?
Did you not see the old folks left alone?
Did you not hear nature keening over you
through the crying of birds and the North Wind?

Your breasts that swelled with abundant milk,
your vigorous wholesome mountain body,
as you leaned far over the rocky hollow
did it not say *no* to you, did it not oppose you?

The sun set and with it the vision of you,
but I stood fixed as stone before the sacred mountain,

and for long I felt deeply throbbing within me
the warmth of your blood, the freshness of your hair,

Women of Suli! Where your bodies are one with the rocks,
the stony earth is adorned with wild flowers,
but on the peak there blooms a single lily to honor
the last Suli woman, foam of your fragrance.

ANGELOS SIKELIANOS

1884–. Born in Lekkas, Ionian Islands. He came to Athens to attend college but left his studies to devote himself to poetry. With the help of his American wife, Eva Palmer, he recreated the Delphic Idea. In the Delphic Festivals of 1927-1930 they presented in the ancient theatre of the Delphic Sanctuary, Prometheus Bound *and* The Suppliants *of Aeschylus. His poetical works are:* Alaphroiskiotos (the Seer) *a vision of his own island and its people (1907),* Verses *(1916),* Prologue to Life *(1915-1920) in five volumes:* Consciousness of My Earth, Consciousness of My People, Consciousness of My Faith, Consciousness of Personal Creation, Easter of the Greeks; Dedication *(1927)* Mother of God, Ionian Rhapsodies, Orphic Poems, The Delphic Word, Poems of Victory, Memorial Poems, 18 Poems of Resistance *(written during the German occupation). These and other lyrics are collected in* Lyrical Life, *in three volumes. Poetical dramas:* Dithyramb of the Rose *(translated into English by Frances Sikelianou),* The Sibyl *(English by Eva Sikelianou),* Daedalus in Crete *(English by Eva Sikelianou),* Christ in Rome *and* Digenis *(English by Eva Sikelianou). Prose works:* Proanakrousna *(the Awakener) and many essays. A number of his poems have been translated into French. He was nominated for the Nobel Prize in 1947.*

ACHELOOS (the river-god)

The White River was flooded, and I, in the midst
of its terrifying surge,
set my legs firm as columns, and over them my body erect
like an opposing God . . .

And suddenly my struggle became an unknown thirst,
and as I opened my lips
to bend a little and drink, the river became a prodigal stream
swirling into my heart.

And the lighter my heart grew, the sweeter I felt
the struggle of my limbs,
and I drank as the breeze of dawn the current that at first
had pounded on my knees.

At last, as the foam thins out when the wave ebbs
on the stretch of sand,
the river bed was left stone dry, and my legs
light as feathers, were free to run!

Then as I enjoyed greater freedom, a lavish boldness
wakened in my breast,
and the freshness of creation and the mountain grandeur
poured all through me . . .

Oh, how much mightier was the dream than the deed
of the demi-god
who, waiting in ambush, seized in his hand the horns of
the bull-shaped river,

and pressing his knee on the double folds of its neck,
broke one horn thus,
and maddened by pain, it rushed into the sea
roaring incessantly . . .

THE STYGIAN OATH

I might have been like the migratory eagles
who can fly to India, Egypt and Greece,
in the course of one spring.

ANGELOS SIKELIANOS

My steps might sometimes have been
like those of seamen, who after sailing the ocean for years
still feel its mountainous billows under foot.

And I might have all at once,
feeling behind me the raven of Acheron
panting to overtake me,
prepared myself
ready to rush forth
beyond the circle of all the closed rhythms of the world,
to seek my destiny from the darkness,
(the full destiny of the poet).

Why, then, did I postpone the great step?

Now I say that you have shown me the road
advancing with dancing steps into the darkness,
immortal warriors,
and that near you
the darkness of death is like the shade
of a great tree, where stretched out close to one another
we talked about Greece as you saw her in that hour
when your eyes were closing on this world—
the world that was crumbling that she might arise afresh
illumined by your fiery spirit.
Now I speak with you,
my dead brothers of the mountain, the sea and the field,
about the shape of a new life to come
in the light of your sacrifice, my brothers!

And again, I might have been like the migratory eagles,
who can fly over India, Egypt and Greece
in the course of one spring.

My steps might sometimes have been
like those of seamen who after sailing the ocean for years
still feel its mountainous billows under foot.

And I might have all at once,
feeling behind me the raven of Acheron
panting to overtake me,
gathered all my strength,
ready to rush forth
beyond the circle of all the closed rhythms of the world
to ask for my destiny from the darkness
(the full destiny of the poet).

Henceforth, I shall not leave your side,
not for a moment do I want to leave your side,
for I have made my heart a threshing-floor
for you to dance on, my warrior-heroes.
I drop my lids and I watch you
entering the mystic dancing floor of death
one by one, hand in hand
and I look at you with eyes closed,
and I still crave, I still crave to gaze on you,
immortal warriors, my brothers,
ever dancing the klephtiko and syrto
on my heart!
From now on I shall never leave your side
even if all the stars
rang out my destiny
(the full destiny of the poet).

But here I leave my heart to you,
a mystic dancing floor,
a huge funeral pyre of the dead,
at once a garden and a cemetery;
until, dancing the klephtiko and syrto deep within it,
one day you too will break its bonds
in one great pulse of joy,
your pulse

in a single recurring rhythm of dance,
your dance—
the eternal dance of Greece!

LETTER FROM THE FRONT

I write to you . . . And yet, so great is the silence
surrounding me,
that I say, if I opened my lips you would hear my voice . . .

Up to yesterday the cannon kept booming
like lions roaring about the summits
in wild slaughter, and over us steely
vultures whirled, incessantly whirling,
casting the shadow of death, holding
death in their claws . . .

But of all things
most awful is the silence that follows
the battle, as deep within us
the wall separating life and death
crumbles and our naked souls,
seeing the living and the dead
all wrapped in a single shroud,
the shroud of the snow, expect
no awakening as before, but some
loud trumpeted resurrection,
a resurrection on horizons that formerly
awakening, we had not lived . . .

And do you
think that up here we cling to dim
traces of time or that our soul is concerned

whether sometime the snows will melt,
whether we are to return to the same
spring that we knew? . . .

As we pass from one
height to the other, the enemy crawls
in the chasm, but now we have reached
a summit which I tell you faces
the future . . . For, truly, whether ours
or the enemy's, each day the cannons
demolish the narrow horizons before us,
and our thoughts, like our bayonets, extend
our borders . . . So tonight, as I stood
on guard like a shepherd,
a flock of clouds about me, (if you should
ask me if it were sunset or noon
I could not tell), a sudden ray
pierced the distance. When it first
was reflected on my bayonet, it gilded
whole peaks, uncovered
the depths of the abyss, valleys,
waters, rivers. But over all,
as if a broad sword were passing through my heart,
it turned back the ray all at once
from the peaks of new life to the cares
of all of you remaining down below,
in secret anxiety awaiting
spring from us . . . For woe to us,
if you expect a spring like those of the past
and not the spring I say will come
carrying a two-edged sword, coming
on the wings of Victory, winnowing out
the chaff from among you,
to receive her . . .

ANGELOS SIKELIANOS

And this is what makes me
write to you at this hour, friend,
to ask: "Are you or are you not ready
to receive such a Spring?"

Perhaps
you will say some may expect her
as I describe her, snatched from the furnace
of battle, glowing from battles
like melted copper with her belt
girdled for war, with eyes
aflame, and on her lips
the language of the people, asking for an answer
in the same language from all of you . . .

So you
may answer: Some expect her,
and for him who is ready the miracle
of her strength may descend all at once.
Just as now while I write,
a tiny little bird flew down,
I do not know from where, facing me, on the enemy
barbed wire that yesterday we cut
to pass to the other side,
and stayed only a moment, and left
a moment's song. It seemed the song poured
everywhere, reached everywhere, spread
Truth everywhere, deep in the world . . .

But the other? Are there many others down there?
Those, who in their warm beds
tremble if they dream of the snow,
but suddenly leap like ghosts

from their thick bedding to hide in
their sham grave, to save

a miserable life whose horizons
are no wider than this grave?
Those who tremble when the people speak
as at a shriek from a siren?
Tell me friend . . .
But no . . . but no . . . I know what you will say:
*Naked spirit! Stench on the sword washed
in the cowardly blood of the foe! Victory,
victory over scarecrows in all the world . . . Terror,
yes, terror to phantoms! . . .*

*Greece
will return to find Greece!*
Friend, farewell!

KLEISOURA

No more words,
no vain, threadbare words used in epics!

Only with your bayonet;
with your bayonet and with your soul,
with your bayonet and with my soul,
both naked,
let us rush forth holding hand in hand,
to our exalted, valiant dance
for the assault of the height!

Henceforth the only fitting word is the one
that first sprang from your indomitable breasts
as our foe appeared before us:
"Aera! Aera!"
But even that is silent in this solitary zone
where higher than the cliffs and snows and rocks,

ANGELOS SIKELIANOS

we sense something enthroned on the great peak,
something that tomorrow will be ours,
ours forever!

Yes, I know it; all around the snow is falling, falling;
wild swirling winds blow from all sides
as if determined to drag us into the chasms.
The abyss yawns gaping at our feet;
our every step slips on the ice
toward the fathomless depths
from where there is no returning;
but we are held together,
hand in hand, poet, soldiers, evzones,
and we go to make something our own,
something that tomorrow will be ours forever!

What is it, men, that lifts us to the summit?
Why, until yesterday, while climbing, was our heart-beat
not even as loud as when it beat at some dance
of one of our feasts near the trumpet,
or near the sound of a viol,
playing with the sweet entrancing bazouki?
What is that shining on high,
like a star ever striving to break through the clouds,
like an infant struggling to get out of its swaddling clothes,
up there, up there,
on the highest peak of Kleisoura.

What is it, my men, my comrades, my eagles, my brothers?
You yourselves do not know how to name it! . . .
But that is why I am with you at this hour,
as you march mutely on your way
nights, days and days and nights again,
undressed, unwashed, unshaved, sleepless, as if you were
weeds of Nature herself surrounding you,

like phantoms of the mountain that seem to climb with you.
That is why I am with you,
only to tell you what is the name
of the star struggling to break through the clouds,
of the infant striving to escape its swaddling clothes,
to tell you quickly only its name.

Up there it is still naked
without blood or flesh,
with heart opened for ages,
with hands bound,
with head bowed bitterly on its chest,
while around the vultures whirl, constantly whirl,
as the sleepless vulture whirled around
the hero, bound to the peaks of the Caucasus,
the Spirit of Man crucified on the heights!
And now you are like Heracles
who ages ago
returning from Hades
resembled you, my brothers;
fasting, bony, with a beard
matted round his face,
like a savage, a ghost, a demigod,
with all his chest, his mind, his knees,
filled with his hidden sleepless struggle,
lifted above the shadow of fear or death,
to deliver the Hero.
So you now,
go to deliver the Spirit of Man,
seeking liberators like yourselves,
liberators who offer their lives
like a single libation of their hearts.
Now as you too go to deliver
the great Exile,

you cut a road through fathomless chasms,
through storms and snows,
through blind nights,
through pitiless blasts in the chaos of the North!
and through your own blood
and your own flesh,
to donate blood and flesh,
to give new life
to the long-suffering spirit,
the Spirit of Man, my brothers!

There, I have given you the name!
Other words now are vain!
This is enough,
enough, from now on, other words, my brothers,
are threadbare, vain words found in any epic!

RESISTANCE

This is not a struggle on marble threshing-floors,
with Digenis standing there and death before him . . .
Here the whole earth rises, with its dead,
and with death itself, it tramples on death . . .

High up on the mountains, and on their peaks,
Resurrection suddenly blazes, a great blast of sound ex-
                                              [plodes . . .
Greece leads the dance high up with the guerrillas,
—the dance has thousands of turns, thousands of tables,
and the dead on the opposite mountains are first revellers!

MARCH OF THE SPIRIT

As I threw the last log on the hearth,
(log of my life locked in time),
on the hearth of your new Liberty, Greece,
my soul suddenly blazed as if space
were all copper, or as if I had
the sacred cell of Heraclitus around me,
where for years,
for eternity, he forged out his thoughts
and hung them as weapons
in the temple of Epheseus . . .

Gigantic thoughts,
like fiery clouds or red islands
in a fabulous sunset,
flamed in my mind,
for all at once my whole life was burning
in the care of your Liberty, Greece!
That is why I did not say:
This is the light of my funeral pyre . . .
I cried, I am the torch of your history!
And there, let my desolate carcass burn like a torch,
Empyrean vine-shoot,
with this torch
walking erect till the last hour,
to light at last all corners of the earth,
to pave a road into the soul,
into your mind, your body, Greece!
I spoke and I paced
bearing my enflamed liver
in your Caucasus,
and each step of mine
was my first and it was I believed my last,

for my bare feet waded in your blood,
for my bare feet stumbled among your corpses,
for my body, my face, my whole mind,
was mirrored as in a lake, in your blood!

There in such a red mirror, Greece,
a fathomless mirror, abysmal mirror
of your liberty and your thirst, I saw myself
heavy with red earth, moulded clay,
a new Adam of the newest creation
we will mould for you, Greece!

And I said:
I know, yes, I know, even your Olympian
Gods have now become a nether foundation,
for we buried them deep—deep so strangers will not find them.
And the whole foundation is doubly and triply fortified
with all the remains our enemies heaped upon it . . .
And I even know that for the libations and the vow
of the new Temple we dreamed for you, Greece,
days and nights, more comrades were slaughtered among them
than lambs were ever slain for Easter! . . .

Fate, and your fate my own to the very depths!
And through love, through great creative love
see how my soul has hardened, hardened and now
enters entire in your mud and your blood, to form
the new heart needed in your new struggle, Greece!
The new heart already locked in my breast,
and today I cry out with her to all comrades:

"Forward, help to lift the sun over Greece!
Forward, help to lift the sun over the world!
For see, his wheel is stuck deep in the mud,
and ah, see, his axle is buried deep in the blood!
Forward, boys, it isn't easy for the sun to rise alone,

push with knee and chest to get him out of the mud,
push with chest and knee to get him out of the blood,
See, we lean on him, we his blood brothers!
Forward brothers, he encircles us with his fire,
forward, forward, we are wrapped in his flame!

Forward creators! . . . Support your burden-bearing impulse
with head and foot, so the sun will not sink!
And help me too, brothers, not to sink with him . . .
For now he is over me, within and around me,
for now I spin in a sacred vertigo with him! . . .

A thousand bulls' rumps support the base;
a two-l eaded eagle shakes its wings
over me and its flapping whirrs
beside my head and in my soul,
and the far and the near for me now are one! . . .
Newly heard, heavy harmonies encircle me! Forward, com-
help him to rise, so the sun may become Spirit!   [rades

The new word is nearing that will dye all
in its new flame, mind and body, pure steel . . .
Our earth has fattened enough from human flesh . . .
Fat and fertile, let us not allow our earth
to harden from this deep blood-bath,
richer, deeper than any first rain!
Tomorrow each one of us must go out with twelve pairs of
to till this blood-drenched soil . . .   [oxen,
For the laurel to blossom on it and become a tree of life,
and our Vine to spread to the ends of the earth . . .

Forward *boys, the sun cannot rise alone . . .*
Push *with knee and chest to get him out of the mud;*
push *with chest and knee, to get him out of the blood;*
push *with hand and head, for the sun to flash as Spirit!"*

So, when I threw the last log on the hearth,
(log of my life locked in time),
on the hearth of your new Liberty, Greece,
my dread cry suddenly took new breath
as if space were all copper, or as if I had
the sacred cell of Heraclitus around me,
where for years,
for eternity, he forged out his thoughts
and hung them as weapons
in the Temple of Ephesus
as I called you comrades!

THE SACRED WAY

Through the new wound that fate opened in me
I felt the setting sun piercing my heart,
like the sudden surge of the wave
entering through a gash
in a ship rapidly sinking . . .
For at last that evening,
like a man long sick who first comes out
to milk life from the outside world,
I was a solitary walker on the road
that starts from Athens,
and has Eleusis as its sacred goal.
For this road always was for me
like the road of the soul . . . flowing
like a great manifest river:
wagons slowly drawn by oxen,
full of haystacks or logs, and other
carriages quickly passing
with the people inside them like shadows . .
But farther on, as if the world were lost

and nature alone were left, little by little
a stillness settled . . . And the rock
I saw rooted at the edge,
appeared like a throne the centuries
had destined for me. And as I sat,
I crossed my hands around my knees, forgetting
whether I had started that day or whether I had taken
this same road centuries ago . . .

But see; from the nearest circle, in this quiet,
three shadows appeared.
One was a gypsy coming toward me,
and behind him, dragged by chains
followed two slow-moving bears.

And see; in a little while as they came near me
and the gypsy saw me, before I could look at him well,
he pulled his tambourine from his shoulder,
and, striking it with one hand,
with the other dragged the chains
violently. And then the two bears
rose up heavily on their hind legs . . . The one,
(clearly it was the mother), the large one,
her brow all adorned with a braid of blue beads
and over it a white amulet to ward off the evil eye,
suddenly raised herself with majesty,
as if she were a wooden idol of the Great Goddess,
centuries old, of the eternal Mother,
of the same one who in sacred sorrow,
in the course of time, as she took human form,
here was named Demeter, pining for her daughter,
and there named Alcmene, or the Virgin,
pining for her son.
And the little bear beside her,
like a big toy, a small ignorant child,

ANGELOS SIKELIANOS

raised itself also, obeying,
but not yet foreseeing
the length of its pain, and the bitterness
of the slavery his mother mirrored
looking at it with her two fiery eyes!

But being exhausted, she was slow
in starting to dance and the gypsy,
with an adroit pull of the chain
on the little one's nostril, still bleeding
from the metal that evidently had pierced it
a few days before, made the mother
groaning with pain, suddenly stand up,
bend her head towards her child,
and begin a wild dance . . .

And I, as I looked on, proceeded
out of time, far from time,
free from forms locked in time,
free from statues and icons;
I was outside, I was outside of time . . .
But before me, forced up by the violence
of the metal ring, and her yearning love,
I saw nothing else but the majestic bear,
with the blue beads on her head,
a monstrous symbol of martyrdom
of the whole world, present and past,
a monstrous symbol of martyrdom
of all ancient pain, whose tax of the soul
is still unpaid by the mortal centuries . . .
for the soul was and still is in Hell . . .
And I kept
my head continuously bent,
as I threw a drachma into the tambourine,
for I too was a slave of the world . . .

But at last, as
the gypsy went ahead, again
dragging the two slow-moving bears,
and was lost in the twilight, my heart
lifted me to take again the road
ending at the ruins
of the sanctuary of the soul at Eleusis.
And as I walked, my heart groaned:
"Will the hour never come,
when the soul of the bear and the gypsy,
and my soul, that I call initiate,
will feast together?"
And as I went on
and night fell, again through the same
wound that fate had opened in me I felt
the darkness surging into my heart
as the wave rushes suddenly through a gash
in a ship rapidly sinking . . .
And yet it was as if my heart thirsted
for such a flood when it sank
totally drowned in the darkness,
totally drowned in the darkness.
A murmur spread over me,
a murmur
and it seemed to say:
"The hour will come!"

DAEDALUS IN CRETE (excerpt)

(Daedalus speaks, quoting Orpheus.)

"In our darkness the sun is a lamp
and the moon a compassion in our loneliness . . .

But the black night sends her charity abundantly . . .
For sometimes she draws the soul from our body
during sleep, like a sword from the scabbard,
sometimes in mystic wakefulness she summons us above
to measure ourselves with the abyss . . . Comrades,
before the light dawns and traps us in its nets,
ah! if only in the opening and shutting of an eyelid,
let us see into the darkness . . . for woe to us,
these are not yet eyes, they are only holes
in our skulls, and Apollo has sunk his roots
higher than all the stars! . . .
Only dedicate all your strength to the darkness,
for the sun arrives and fishes for your souls
with golden nets and the moon comes up,
and you waste your mind in dreams;
but your mind has roots in the ether,
it must break the golden nets of the sun
and seize its own source beyond dreams!"

KOSTAS VARNALIS

1884—. Born in Pyrgo, Bulgaria. He studied in Philopopoulos and at the University of Athens. He was appointed a teacher of Greek literature in Bulgaria, then at the Pedagogic Academy in Athens. He studied philosophy, philology and fine arts as well as modern Greek literature as a government fellowship student of Sociology at Paris. Poetic works include: Honeycomb, The Light That Burns *(1933),* The Castrated People, Slaves Besieged *(1927—banned by the Metaxas dictatorship for a short while),* The Living People, The Lament of Penelope. *In 1925, the Pagalos dictatorship dismissed him from his post because of his books. He published a critical work about Dionysios Solomos entitled* Solomos Without Metaphysics. *He also wrote* The True Apology of Socrates, *a parody of the Apology of Socrates. Many of his poems have been published in the Alexandrian magazine* Grammata.

THE PAINS OF THE VIRGIN MARY

Where can I hide you, my dear son, so that evil men will not
On what ocean island, on what desolate peak?   [reach you?
I will not teach you to protest and cry out against wrong,
for I know that your heart will be so kind, so sweet,
that soon you will writhe in the nets of wrath.

You will have blue eyes, a tender body,
I will guard you from the evil eye and from bad weather,
from the first shock of awakened youth.
You are not for strife, you are not for the cross,
you are a real man, not a slave or traitor.

I will awake at night, walk slowly on tip-toe,
bend to hear your breath, my little warm bird,
make ready on the fire milk and camomile,
and then through the window, with loud heart-beat I'll watch
you carrying slate and pencil on your way to school . . .

And if sometime the Lord of heaven should strike your mind
with truth, a flash of light, my little child do not reveal it.
Men are such monsters, they cannot stand the light.
There is no truth more golden than the truth of silence.
If you were born a thousand times, so often would they put
                                              [you on the cross.

DOOMED

In a basement tavern,
amid smoke and swearing,
(up above the organ grinding),
the whole crowd was drinking last night,
last night like every other evening,
to wash down the poisons of life.
Pressed against his fellow,
someone spat on the floor.
"Oh! what great torment
is the torment of life!
No matter how the mind is tried,
it can't recall a bright day!"

(Sun and azure sea
and the deep of the prodigal sky;
oh, the yellow gauze of dawn,
carnations of sunset
you shine, fade far away,
without entering our hearts!)

For ten years this one's father
is a spectre-like paralytic;
this other man's almost lifeless wife
melts consumptive in the house.
Mazi's son in Palamidi dungeon,
Yavi's daughter in a Gazi brothel.

Our blundering fate is to blame!
God who hates us is to blame!
Our stupid brain is to blame!
First of all the wine is to blame!
Who is to blame? Who is to blame? No mouth
has uttered it and said it yet.

So in the dingy tavern,
cringing, we always drink,
every heel steps on us
as if we were worms.
Cowards, doomed and undecided,
maybe we are waiting for a miracle!

THE MOTHER OF CHRIST

How the streets smell sweetly strewn with palms,
sun-stepped streets and flower-beds all around!
The joy of the festival continues to swell.
Afar it moans, it ascends afar.

Sea of people, wave upon wave, your joy
was fed for long on your hatred of others.
If your black malice thirsted for sin,
at last it found its victim, an innocent one!

Ah! How I too like a mother was fearful
(it was a dream that remained, mist that faded)!

Would that I had given birth to you as to your other brothers,
far from glories and far from hate!

A red house in a yard with a well . . .
and a vine arbour full of amber clusters of grapes . . .
A kind head of the house returning each night,
the golden night calm and sweet as the oil.

And when you opened the door with saws in hand,
your clothes covered with fine shavings,
(white beard, white hands) your wife, a dove,
breathed deeply the air filled with cedar.

And when you had stayed awhile and the house filled
with your good shadow, Father and Master,
your only daughter coming out to pour water for you,
the impatient dinner would start with laughter.

Death for the aged would be sweet.
You would leave many offspring, sons and grandsons,
a flock for each, a field and a vine,
a workshop for that one who wanted your trade.

I lower the black kerchief down to my eyes,
so my mind may cease seeing with the eyes . . .
The nightingales revel in the gardens round,
the fine aroma of the lemon trees surrounds you.

You go away in the springtime, my son, my darling,
my sweet spring, without returning.
Your beauty faded yellow, my son.
You did not speak, see my sweet, how I wither.

As the cow moans when they seize her child,
I screamed and the words made no sense.
Open your two large eyes for me,
my breasts drip blood where you suckled milk.

How could your heart have been so unwise,
to come like a Caesar to renowned Jerusalem!
Though the mobs cheered madly (woe to you!)
They did not even know your name!

Near-by your enemies bit their lips . . .
Cunningly they aroused the thoughtless mobs;
by the time the sun went down and dusk had come,
your foes and friends had nailed your cross.

Why did you let them take you?
When they asked, "Who is Jesus?" why did you say, "Here
Ah! My bitter mouth does not know what it is saying! [I am?"
Thirty years my child; I do not know you yet.

THE BALLAD OF ANDREW

The boat of hunchback Andrew
had a fringed awning,
crouched at the edge of the boat,
he always saw beautiful visions.

Catherine and Zoe,
little Antigone, Zenobia,
(was life a dream?
Poor heart, how loudly you beat)

On hot noons,
all the girls together,
took Andrew's boat,
and slowly rowed out to the open sea.

Suddenly they would fall into the water,
each a naked mermaid,
and Andrew's eye
grew smaller and smaller, a pointed needle.

"God is almighty,"
his bitter lip said.
"He is mighty and good,
and his golden gifts are plenteous."

But the evil winter came
and the mad party scattered,
and a hidden pain
felled you, good Andrew.

And though you spat blood into the sea,
Zenobia passed before you.
(the hand organ was playing a soft song
at the tavern.)

She asked how you were managing
the many worries of your life.
"Take this little money
to get well and start anew!"

And the boat, a laughing mother,
rocked you slowly, always with love,
and you rested forever, Andrew,
crouched at the edge of the boat.

How great is God,
the Father, the Son, and the Holy Ghost!

THE "GOOD" PEOPLE

I came from the village
with my whole family.
What a relief to my heart!
Now my belly can be filled!
Draw a lot, throw the dice,
see who will win.

Leap, supple girl
to bag-pipes and flutes!
Since you are ripe and mature,
you'll be harvested this year;
a man will fetch and take you
with horse, buggy and priest.

The flame of the wine constricts us,
a lump in the throat.
Folks and dogs
howl as loud as they can.
Old and young women
lift their skirts high as they can.

Death raises
your sapless limbs
pale and emaciated
on his cold pitchfork.
I prick you with the reed;
you do not yield a drop of water.

How soon you expired!
You have spoiled our feast.
Where is your grandeur,
the warmth of your fancy?
You were a God and a king
with the soul of a fly!

They destroyed the churches
and re-built them in a minute!
Then wake up, since stones,
mud, the knout strike you!
Come on, wash and comb yourself
let's see some action!

Join hands with us and dance;
drink foamy ritsina,

and Egypt and Bagdad
will become your domains.
I will even hire for you
a servant girl named Spiridoula.

Your hard-working ancestors
gave birth to you in dung,
and yet you sought as your kingdom,
the earth and the heavens!
Like the proverbial bishop of Damalas,
now you're in for it!

No bronze armour,
no infantry and cavalary,
no ships on the seas,
no blood-stained pistol-belt;
starving and barefooted,
behold the absolute monarch!

You seemed a quiet lad.
Why did you take the wrong road,
attack the Faith on the one hand,
and righteous law on the other.
Only two things count
custom and Holy Writ!

Were you a klepht on the mountains,
a murderer in the city,
a spy and false witness,
all would have honored you.
As Barabas, you too
would be pardoned for everything.

(a woman in her thin passionate voice)

I used to lean out the window
to water the potted plant

as you passed proudly by,
eye firm, footstep direct.
Now, naked and good,
once I spit, once I laugh at you.

(again, altogether)

I pay my taxes to the State
and I am not in arrears.
My last obols
I put in the church tray.
What my ancestors have bequeathed
goes from child to grandchild.

Outside gilded palaces
my heart passes and quakes.
Indoors a sultan and pasha,
with a large harem,
songs, incense,
wonders of Arabian Nights.

My eye shed no tear
nor was my mind scandalized,
all these things are temporary,
according to the Faith.
I walk the narrow road
to the joys of Paradise.

Without inequality,
how justice would flourish!
Without holy war
how goodness would grow!
Prudent, conventional
I follow the victor.

And since sometimes they take from me
shack and farm,

the immature girl—
her mother's treasure,
I will find them on high, everyone,
and Evangelo still a virgin!

. . . .

Come wife, night has fallen,
gather in the basket,
bottles, bread and cheese.
Take the children by the hand,
move aside, lest I take a shot at you,
I'm going to make a double-shot.

The point of this lesson
will always enlighten,
People are a swarming bee-hive
when annoyed.
One thing is certain:
Drowsiness and Custom.

MARKOS AVGERIS

1884—. Pseudonym for George Papadopoulo. Born in Yanina. Specialized in medicine in Athens. His play, Before the People, *was produced in Athens.* Song of the Table *is a collection of verse. He has written many critical studies and translations from the ancient Greek.*

GRANNY TASSIA

When the foe came in numbers,
they seized the fine fort,
dragged boys and girls away as slaves,
stole whole stacks of silver,
but it's Yan that the enemy wants,
and Yan fights them off in his house.
Round and round the house they go,
and still he holds them off.
Near him his old mother Tassia,
puts on her Sunday clothes,
while his young wife, Maro,
at the icon makes a cross,
and his daughter, Dawn, his star,
on her knees, offers prayers.

When she has donned her clothes,
Granny Tassia speaks to her son:
"Listen Yanos, my son.
Do not let them dishonour your dear ones;
you have a wife still young,
and a very youthful daughter.
With a knife-thrust end our lives,
then set fire to the house,

and at the break of dawn,
throw yourself into the fighting."

"Pronounce a blessing, Mother!"
"With all my soul, my son."

Then into her breast the old woman
received the blade of the knife,
and Maro, his young wife,
offered her white neck
near her two gold coin necklaces,
beneath her golden hair,
and in her hands, Dawn, his star,
held her weeping face,
and with her ardent prayer
her white soul fled.
Where Tassia was slain,
they have built a church;
and where Maro was slain
the young folks dance;
and where Dawn lies,
grow lilies of the field.

PLEBEIAN SONG

Noble nature is the essence of nobility . . .
So it seems rather to belong within my breast
where I feel the life force swelling . . .
Though they say the Plebeian kind is vile,
I enjoy the sight of my sunny children
and I give my full breast to the hungry throng.
Such a treasure of nobility I have in my breast
it surpasses the finely carved bed of the grand patrician lady.

NICHOLAS KAZANTZAKIS

1885—. Born in Candia, Crete. Studied law at the University of Athens, philosophy in Paris, literature and art in Germany and Italy. His first book was a novel: The Serpent and the Lily. *His first play* The Dawn Shines *won for him the prize of the year awarded by the University of Athens, as did his second play* The Overseer. Kapodistrias, *a historical drama was selected for production on Greek Independence Day. Works in philosophy:* Neitszche and the Philosophy of Right, Bergson, Mount Sinai, China and Japan. *Drama:* The Dawn Shines, Christ, Odysseus, The Overseer, Nicephorus Phocas, The Trilogy of Prometheus, Yangtse, Melissa, Kapodistrias, Julian the Apostate. *Poetry:* The Odyssey. *Novels:* The Serpent and the Lily, Broken Souls, Zorbas, Toda Raba *(published in Spanish and Dutch). Translations: Goethe's* Faust, The Divine Comedy, *etc. In 1947 he was proposed by the Hellenic Literary Organization for the Nobel Prize.*

THE ODYSSEY

(This is an original treatment of the Odysseus story and includes various post-Homeric legends in which Odysseus resumes his wanderings after his return to Ithaca and liberation of Penelope from her suitors.)

A—Lines 74-123 *(Odysseus had killed the suitors)*

When he had cut down the ardent youth in his spacious courts,
Odysseus hung up his long, glutted bow,
and stepped into the warm bath to wash his mighty body.
Two female slaves poured water, but when they saw the
[master,

they shrieked for his curly-haired belly and loins steamed,
and thick black blood dripped from both his palms;
and the bronze pitchers rolled knocking on the flagstones.
The long-wandering one laughed serenely into his curling
[beard,
and upping his brows he signed to the maidens to go.
Long he enjoyed the tepid water and the veins of his body
expanded like rivers and his loins were refreshed;
and his great mind cleared and relaxed in the water.
Now soothed, he rubbed gently with aromatic oil
his brine-toughened body and his long hair;
and young attendants came and his weathered flesh bloomed.
On gold-headed nails, in the perfumed shade,
hung gleaming the chitons his trusted wife had woven
with ships embroidered and gods and swift winds.
He stretched his great sun-darkened hand and leisurely chose
the brightest one and flung it flat over his shoulder,
and in a cloud of vapor, he drew the bolt and crossed the
[threshold.
The slaves looked burnished in the shade and the smoked
of the ancestral mansion reflected the leaping fire;   [beams
and Penelope pale and mute, waiting beside the throne,
turned to view him and her knees were shaken with terror:
"Oh gods, this is not the man I yearned for long years.
Here is a forty-span monster walking the house as a man!"
His arrow-sharp brain divined the sombre dread
of the wretched lady and slowly he communed with his un-
[derstanding heart:
"My heart, this is the wife who waited for you downcast for
[years,
to part her locked knees and enjoy the ecstasy together.
This is the woman you craved while battling seas
and the gods, and the deep voices of your immortal mind!"
Thus he spoke, but his heart did not leap in his great breast.

His nostrils still steamed from the heat of the recent slaughter;
and he studied his wife in the midst of the tangled young
[bodies,
and looking askance, his keen watchful eye clouded, almost
stabbing her with his sword at the peak of the slaughter.
Swift and silent he walked to the broad threshold.
At last the torrid sun set and the arched storerooms
and recesses filled all around with rose-blue shadows.
In the center of the court smoked the sated black altar to
[Athene
and in the long arcades, livid, their tongues bitten through,
some female slaves swung gently, strung up in the evening
Serenely he gazed at the star-eyed night   [freshness.
descending the mountains with the curly-haired flocks;
dreamily the day's travail of slaughter and the flying arrows
settled like mist in his heart, and soothed,
his tiger heart, glutted, licked itself in the dark.

Odysseus no longer contented with his wife, his son, his old Gods, his land, decided to leave Ithaca. He chose several companions, built a new boat, married his son to Nausicaa, and one morning he spread his sails and went out to sea.

G—Lines 1-34 *(They leave Ithaca)*

The gods sent a thin rain on earth, and sweetly refreshed,
the huge hairy hands seized the oars on the sea.
Silent they turned their faces toward the divine island;
their senses bewitched by the fresh aroma wafted down the
of thyme, vineyards, the ripening grain,   [mountain
by the rock-partridges rushing down to drink,
the misty ravine paths echoing to their drumming.
In the fog sheathed dawn, the thick mist at its feet,
the sacred isle smiled, rosy as an awakening child.

Mountain villages were suspended in light on the slopes,
bells sounded tinkling like the running water
and suddenly, unbearable, deep, full of patience and pain,
so that the earth moaned, they heard the lowing kine.
A steady mainland breeze blew, fluttering the sail
and the painted boat leaped like a huge dolphin,
with the large eyes opened on the foamy prow,
its upflung, sinewy tail dyed blue.
Abruptly, as they rounded the cape, from a rose-resounding
the sweet voice of a woman was heard lifted in song. [cave,
She sang, and the earth-shore, facing the wave,
was sad as a widow, seized by gloomy memories.
But Streidas, chief of the crew, shading his eyes with his palm,
gazed afar at the distant rocks and his heart danced.
In his youth, somewhere such a tune had echoed on the wave,
when first to his house he had brought his mistress wife.
The gods had laughed on the seas, the pebbles smiled,
the sails had filled like the heart of a bridegroom, while the
had sung soft strains at the ornamented prow, [bride,
greeting her husband's new land appearing,
and our bridegroom Streidas had sighed with pleasure and
 [stroked his beard:
"O gods, blow the sea so that we may make port,
enter our little home and close the door behind us!"
Lo now, he hears again the same strains and he almost loses
 [his reason.

Lines 45-54

Unspeaking, Odysseus steered the boat far from the shore,
enfolded the island in his mind, piece by piece,
transplanting houses, mountains, trees, the port,
and all rushed furiously into the funnel of his mind:

from its very bed he uprooted the whole island, and it sank
[into his memory.
As the sea emptied and his country was lost from his sight,
a deep bitterness engulfed him, in his heart he was afraid:
"Comrades, never again shall we see this before our eyes.
It was a small, small bird, it is fled, a toy, a fragment,
a stalk of curly mint that fell from our ear!"

Odysseus began his last great journey. First he anchored in Sparta. When he had saved his old fellow-fighter Menelaos from the insurrectionists, he carried away Helen who felt dissatisfied with the stifling daily life. Now he anchors in Crete, then in the decline of its great civilization.

H—Lines 781-807

Pale on the covered porch the high-born lady reclines
on gold embroidered cushions, on a downy couch,
she broods, a reed dipped in red dye pursed,
she holds smooth mother-of-pearl under her palm,
desolate, filled with her sorrow and ruin, she cuts her bitter
"My heart is trapped in the thick net of the rain; [plaint:
the water lilies sleep and the crocus blooms,
and the earth, like a woman in love, crouches weeping.
O gods, my paint is washed off, my hair uncurled,
my fingers ache from heavy golden rings
and the proud nipples of my breast are faded and fallen.
I lean out pale in the rain and shed my petals like a rose.
Yesterday at dusk a workman crossed the courtyard and water
[dripped
from his towering curly head and his loins steamed;
and I used my eyes sweetly, secretly smiled at him.
But he was awed by the noble adornments on my neck
and the barren golden crown I wear

and prone he stretched on the earth to worship me.
Covered by his body, the courtyard rejoiced in him but my
[heart sank.
O gods, could I but descend with him in the mire!
Misery tugs at me, my hair blows wild,
I lean my breasts to the wind and I tremble under the drops
like a blown white rose lost in the breeze."
When the high-born lady had carefully marked her dismal
[pain on the misty mother of pearl,
she let it hang outside the window in the thin night rain;
and slowly her words of complaint began to fuse, to melt,
and the white wall of the women's apartments reddened as
[with blood.

Battling with the savage tribes in Africa, he reached the source of the Nile. He climbed the mountain alone, joyfully planning the laws of a new city.

X—Lines 1-35

"What joy to climb alone the solitary mountain,
in the clear air, with a laurel leaf stuck between the teeth!
What joy to feel the mighty king of veins playing through the
coursing through the knees, loins, seizing the throat, [legs,
spreading like a river, watering the roots of the brain.
No need to say: "I will go right, I will go left," but to feel
the four winds blow at the crossroads of the brain,
and as you reach the heights, to hear the gods breathing all
[around,
laughing beside you, striding about, rolling the boulders;
to return and see no soul even as the hunter coming out
into the rosy dawn for partridge, spies not even a feather,
but he hears the whole cool mountain thumping!
Oh joy! The earth fluttering like a banner in the morning mist,

a horse your soul rides, strong and swordlike,
double-loined, the head a fortress, and on the broad chest,
the sun and moon suspended like silver-gold beads.
And as you hunt for the unattainable birds, you leave all
 [thought behind,
the clanging din of life, its meretricious joys,
bid farewell to virtue and benumbing love
and, as the rattlesnake sheds his skin on the throne,
you shed the worm-licked earth behind you!
The frivolous in the taverns guffaw and the maidens blush,
while the small house owners shake their bonnets and threat-
 [ening,
covet your fruit, your soul, but they fear the precipice.

He built his new city, he fortified it and engraved on the falls the new proud commandments of his god. He was happy to found a society of free, daring men. But at the celebration on the following day, an earthquake opened the earth and swallowed the city. Odysseus now all alone, battled to conquer fate, no longer believing that gods, virtue or justice exist or rule the world. He had faith only in himself and his five senses.

P—Lines 1209-1245

"There is no longer any tyrant ruling on earth, all hearts are
 [freed!
In the morning the sun-flame rises at my right temple,
all day long it crosses the great dome of my head and sets
at dusk in a red stream at my left temple!
The stars light within me; men, beasts and thoughts graze
in the green short-lived meadow of my mature mind;
laughter and tears press against the corners of my lids,
my mind overflows with dreams, my heart with phantoms—

but when my mind, dark lantern, is snuffed out, all is snuffed
I light fires in the fog, anchor buoys,   [out together.
I open roads in the wind and give order to chaos;
five slave weavers in the loom of my mind
weave and unweave life in the ribbed fabric of the air;
I cover the whole abyss with a coarse partridge-coloured cloth,
whereon I embroider my house, I beget my sons,
I put trust in the wheat seed and I tie my horse,
and I build my life sparsely for it is a flash in the fog.
I puff at it gently and all disappears and my heart goes forth,
without anger or condescension, without longing or hope,
small lightning with many colored wings piercing the night!
Ah, ancestor, crouched on the other side of the shore shooting
                                                [your arrows,
with your favor I have excelled you, and from the forest of
                                                [the brain,
I return in the evening singing and I carry the corpse
of deer-like Hope, with her large weeping eyes!
I set my cap jauntily, walk the earth with music
and the fire ascends and seizes my hair like a crown!"
The inspired solitary is silent and his body glows
like a volcanic flame at the crater's lips reflected on the stone;
and the mind, armed like a scorpion, promenades on live
                                                [embers.
The people are frightened and shade their faces from the sun;
and again over the precipices is heard the aged alluring voice;
"By the three hundred and sixty-five joints binding my body,
by the three hundred and sixty-five vipers belting my soul,
no god exists nor ruler, nor virtue nor Justice!
nor reward in heaven, nor punishment in hell!"
The solitary spoke and his laughter rang out joyously as if a
                                                [spring
had suddenly gushed from the earth and spouted to the sun.

Odysseus began his last journey where he ultimately met Death. In his wanderings he saw all the great leaders who brought to mankind new ideas, religions, and measured himself against them. He continued his road alone to the south. At Africa's tip, he saw Death come to meet him in his silent vessel. The cold reached out to Odysseus, an iceberg finally overturned his frail craft. The great hero conquered at last by the insuperable forces of nature succumbed, first offering thanks to his five senses for having served him so well, and then playing final homage to the never setting sun—Healer and Destroyer at the same time.

PSI—Lines 1-36

O Sun, who art father, mother and son, my three-masted good!
You lie on the earth with our fine women, O begetter,
and if you do not shoot seed into their sacred wombs,
the womb is empty and sterile and there is no offspring.
You are our mother, too, the strong breast overflowing with
and all mouths await you, all lips open   [milk,
bright and early in the light to hang on the breast, sweetly to
                                                   [suckle!
Sun, it is you who cover the eggs in the nest with your own
You peck at the shell with your golden beak, [warm feathers.
and within, the embryo bores its way, stirs and answers;
and gently the mid-wall breaks, the shells break open
and the birds pour into your embrace, Sun, for you to feed!
You are a son and you play on the waters, you roll on the
                                                   [grass,
when you hunger, you hang on our breasts, you turn blood
my son, and as you wake at dawn, a fiery ball,   [into milk
a thousand birds awake in our breasts, a thousand cradles
Sun, thrice beloved.supreme delight of our mortal eyes, [rock!
hold us ever in your palm, hatch us, O god,

and make our feet winged and all the earth into air!
And receive into your caressing embrace this old archer,
do not abandon him alone to the maggots
their secret jaws have started to open on his entrails.
Sun, flood his heart and transform the larvae
into myriads of large, red gold butterflies.
Make Death come, a rider striking boldly,
amid great splendor and heights, amid briny embraces.
Let him come with his sickles and his bare bones
to slavish, meekly loving souls and cowardly heads.
But here it is not fitting; he must come as a lord to knock at
[the gates,
the five famed gates of the fortress and with great respect
whatever in this vigorous body Death could not conquer in
[the mighty struggle,
let it be pure spirit and lightning and laughter and action.
Let him come and loot only the dregs of the body!
O Death, this archer has fooled you, he has laid waste your
[booty,
and you must know, he melted all the rust of the flesh before
[you arrived.
It became spirit and it escaped you and you are only able to
[carry away
extinguished fires and ash and the dregs of the flesh.

He cried out, summoned all his beloved companions and his trusty dog from Ithaca. They heard the voice of the master, Odysseus's boat was again filled.

Odysseus received them joyfully, lifted his hand and gave them the parting signal in a fearless, triumphant voice:

Cast away, my comrades, and propitiously, sweetly, blew the
[breeze of death.

GALATEA KAZANTZAKIS

1886–. Born in Heraklion, Crete. Wrote under pseudonym Petroula Psiloriti. She is primarily known as a short story writer.

SINNER

> "God created man in His own image,
> in the image of God created He him."
> *Genesis 1-27*

In Smyrna, Melpo,
Hero in Salonika,
Katinitsa once in Volo,
now in the Vourla they call me Lela.
Which was my country?
Who were my kin?
God's curse upon me if I know.
My home and country are the brothels.
Even my bitter childhood years
are cloudy, faded scenes.
My memory is an empty chest.
Today is worse than yesterday,
tomorrow will be worse than today.
Kisses from strange mouths, curses,
and the policemen dragging me,
orgies, quarrels till dawn,
diseases, amphitheatre of Syngrou
and injections of 606,
rotten plank of a sunken ship,
all my life wasted,

but from my hell I shout:
Society, I am your mirror, created in your image!

(Vourla—Pireaus red light district.
Syngrou—infirmary in Athens for venereal diseases.)

THE LABORER

I saw the Lord in a field where a humble laborer,
bent over, was making deep furrows with his ancient plow.
He bent with him, his unseen right-hand shield,
while above, the beaming heavens covered them.

Invisible, His grace blessed the laborer's sweat,
which slithered steadily down the deep furrows of his brow
and where it fell, He raised poppies flame like,
swaying indolent, endlessly in the light.

And as the laborer seemed to know the partner of his toil,
for his heart beat quickly with joy,
and as his calm glance rejoiced in the field,
he felt the earth's fragrance deep in his heart.

Again He was with him when tireless he sowed
the plenteous seed, slowly moving his hand,
while soft, soft, the autumn singing rain
watered the parched earth.

And He was there again when the full ears of corn
gushed forth and waved in the soft wind
and when they rustled a golden wave in the sea breeze
and the blade of the scythe mowed down armsful.

When the frugal supper was set in the blessed home,
the wife cutting the brown loaf, said
"Blessed are the labours of my man," and he, with joy in his
rejoiced in the respite of the moment.   [breast

KOSTES OURANIS

1890—. Born in Constantinople, pseudonym of Nearchos. At an early age he devoted himself to poetry as well as to journalism and literary criticism. He published a study of Baudelaire, and his poetic works include: Like the Dreams, Spleen, Nostalgias. Travel Impressions from Spain, Sol Y Sombra, *are prose works.*

PRAYER TO GOD TO REST ALL THE UNFORTUNATE

Oh God, this night of the mournful winter
when your angels in their perennial spring abodes,
lean out over their deserted balconies and look
on earth and slowly strew it with white petals,
as silently it whirls in the infinite;
Oh God, this night, when breezes shout
like sinful souls which the graves reject,
think of those stretched out on one poor bed
sleeping, it seems, only to gather strength
to endure tomorrow too, the pain of yesterday . . .

Oh God, feel with a human heart, and consider this night
first the aged poets who live unknown
because success has never knocked on their door;
consider all of those locked in damp rooms
who try to hold fast to whatever life throws their way
those who have grown tired of living and wait for
a tomorrow, different from others, that they know will not
[arrive.
Consider all who are ugly and mocked by others,
the innocent idiots teased by the world,
the sick who die daily—and go on living,

the young girls who do not have what pleases us—
those who suffer that others might rest,
the quiet and the good, the persecuted
who cannot weep because they have wept so much.
Consider God, all who in this world are doomed
to bow, to crawl and to feel pain without
finding in their churches surcease for that pain
because their thin voices are so cracked
and your throne is so high, so very high . . .

Consider God, all those who suffer without reason
and send them now no happiness as recompense
for no bliss can repay the woes they have had—this night—
when all have shut their eyes in sleep, make
death step gently into their dismal house,
so gently and softly as not to waken them
and lean over them like a sister—not a mother,
because she embraces tightly, a mother holds tight in despair—
let him kiss them on their closed and wrinkled lips
and take with that kiss their breath . . .

Oh God, this night of the mournful winter,
when your angels in their perennial spring abodes,
lean out over their deserted balconies and look
on earth and slowly strew it with white petals,
as silently it whirls in the infinite;
up above to paradise where the blessed go
do not take these dead, but order them buried
so deep within the earth that this world's din
will never reach their sleep—and there let them lie forgotten.

KOSTAS KARIOTAKIS

1896-1928. Born in Tripoli. He was a student of law at the University of Athens, but devoted himself to poetry. Among his works are: The Pain of Men and Things *(1919),* Nepenthes *(1921),* Elegies and Satires *(1927), and translations of Heine, John Moreas, Leopardi. In 1920 he received a prize from the Poetry Brotherhood Contest. He committed suicide at Prevesa on July 20th 1928.*

SLEEP

Shall it be given us to have the luck
to go and die one night
on the green shore of our land?
We will sleep sweetly like children.
The stars and the things of the world
will rise skyward over us.
The wave will caress us like a dream,
and our dream, azure as a wave,
will lead us to lands that do not exist.
The breezes will be loves on our hair,
the breath of the sea-weed will anoint us,
and beneath our wide eyelids
without perceiving it, we will laugh.
The roses will move from the fences
and will come to us as pillows,
to make our sleep a harmony
in which the nightingales will sleep.
We will sleep sweetly like children,
and the girls of our village,
like wild pear trees, will stand all around
and as they bend will whisper to us

of golden cottages, of the Sunday sun,
of the all-white flower pots,
of our fine years that have gone
and as we slowly close our eyes,
the pale old woman, holding our hand,
will unfold for us, like a fairy-tale
the bitterness of life. And the moon
will dip down like a torch at our feet
in the hour of our last sleep.
On the green shore of our land,
we will sleep sweetly like children,
who have cried all day long and are grown weary.

ATHENS

The hour is sweet. Lovely Athens stretches out
yielding to April like a hetaira.
There is voluptuous fragrance in the air—
the soul awaits nothing more.

The silvery eyelids of evening
lower and press over the houses.
Yonder, the Acropolis in royal purple
is a queen, wearing the sunset.

A kiss of light, then the first star bursts,
in Elysium the breeze falls in love
with the quivering rose-laurels, newly wed.

Sweet hour of joy and love when
birds chasing each other
beat the air around an Olympian column.

PREVESA

(the poet committed suicide in Prevesa)

Death is in the crows that flap their wings
on the black walls and brick rooftops.
Death is in the women who make love
as if they were peeling onions.

Death is on the dirty unmentioned roads
with their brilliant long names,
in the olive grove, in the sea all around and even
in the sun—death within deaths.

Death is in the policeman who wraps
and weighs the shortweight portion;
death is in the hyacinth on the balcony,
even in the teacher with the newspaper.

Military base, garrison, regiments of Prevesa—
On Sunday we will hear the band.
I open up a bank account,
and make a deposit of thirty drachmas.

Strolling slowly on the quay
"Am I living?" you ask yourself and you answer, "No."
A boat arrives. The flag is raised.
Perhaps His Honor the Prefect has come.

If at least from among these men
one would die of ennui . . .
silent, mournful, with every sign of respect,
we would all enjoy the funeral.

DIAKOS

One April day
Green glitter—
the field laughed
with the three-leaf clover.

While the morning dazzle
kissed her,
somehow nature
spoke sweetly.

Birds sang
flying about
ever higher.

The flowers were fragrant,
and in wonder, he exclaimed,
"How can I ever die?"

MICHAEL

They drafted Michael into the army.
He started out proudly and grand
with Mario and Panajoti.
But he could not master the manual of arms.
He kept muttering: "Corporal, sir,
let me return to my village."

The next year in the hospital,
silently he stared at the sky.
He riveted his eyes on one spot,
his glance nostalgic and meek,
as if he were saying, as if he were pleading:
"Let me return to my home."

And Michael died as a soldier.
Some few comrades followed him,
Mario and Panajoti among them,
and laid the earth over him,
but they left his feet uncovered.
The poor man was a little too tall.

GEORGIOS SEFERIS

1900–. Born in Smyrna. Attended school in Athens and studied law in Paris. The son of an international lawyer, he joined the diplomatic corps and has been sent to various countries. In 1941 Seferis was in the Middle East with the exiled Greek Government. He has written The Myth of History *and* Strophe. *He translated Byron and T. S. Eliot's* The Waste Land *into modern Greek. He won the Palamas Prize of 1947. Mr. Seferis has been connected with the Greek Embassy at Ankara, Turkey.*

THE CISTERN

Here in the soil a cistern is rooted
haunt of a water secretly hoarded.
Her roof rings with sonorous steps. The stars
do not reach its heart. Each day
lengthens, begins and ends, never touches her.

The world above opens fan-like
and plays with the breath of the wind
with a rhythm expiring at twilight,
hopelessly flapping its wings and throbbing
to the sigh of destined pain.

On the vaulted arch of a pitiless night
cares advance and joys pass by
to the rapid rattle of fate.
Faces light up, gleam a moment,
and fade in an ebony darkness.

Departing faces! Eyes like necklaces
roll in a groove of bitterness
and the traces of broad daylight

take them and bring them closer
to the black earth which seeks no ransom.

The body of man inclines towards the soil
leaving behind his unfulfilled love;
like a stone statue touched by time,
he falls naked on the rich
breast which softens him little by little.

The thirst of love has need of tears,
the roses droop like our soul,
nature's heart-throbs are heard on the leaves.
Dusk approaches like a walker.
Then the night and then the grave . . .

But here in the soil, a cistern is rooted,
warm, secret haunt, hoarding
the groan of each body in the breeze,
the struggle with night, with day.
The world grows, passes, never touches her.

The hours pass by, the suns and the moons,
but the water is grown solid as a mirror;
expectation waits with wide-open eyes
even after all sails sink
at the ends of the sea that feeds it.

Alone, yet such a throng in her heart.
Alone, yet such weariness in her heart.
Alone, yet so much pain in every drop
casting her nets far into the world
that lives in its melancholy wave.

Just as the wave was leaving its confines
would that it might remain confined,
would that it might bring us love

just before breaking its line, at the edge.
The wave foams as it breaks on the sand.

A warmth, spread out like sheep-skin,
calm as the slumbering beast
whose breath ceased peacefully,
knocks at the gates of sleep in search of
the garden where drops of silver fall.

And a secret body, a deep cry
wrung from the grotto of death
alive as the water in the furrow
like the water sparkling on the grass,
conversing alone with the black roots . . .

Ah! closer to the root of our life,
than thought or care!
Ah, closer than our cruel fellow-man
who looks at us through lowered lids
even closer than the spear in our ribs!

Ah! Would that the skin of silence encasing us,
could suddenly soften to our touch,
that we might forget, O gods, the sin
ever spreading and weighing upon us,
that we might escape our thought and our passions!

That we might hug to ourselves the pain of our wound
to escape the pain of our wound,
that we might hug to ourselves the pain of our body,
to escape the body's bitterness,
that roses might bloom in the blood of our wound.

Let all become as it was at first
let us shed the age-old malady
from fingers, lips and eyes
as snakes shed their yellow skins,
on the green clover.

Pure and boundless love, serenity!
One night in the fever of life,
you bent modestly, a nude curve,
a white wing over the flock
like a soft hand on the brow.

The sea that brought you has carried you
far to trees which are in bloom.
Now that the fates have sweetly awakened
a thousand faces with three plain wrinkles
accompany in procession the epitaph.

The myrrh-bearers prolong their dirge
for the hope of man to follow
wedged in the eyes by flames
lighting the blind earth,
which sweats from the travail of spring.

Flames of the world beyond, torches
over the springtime sprouting seed,
mournful shadows on dead wreaths
footsteps . . . footsteps . . . the slow knell
unwinds a sombre chain.

"We die! Our gods are dying . . ."
The statues know it looking on
over the sacrificial victim, like a white dawn,
strange, with lowered lids, in ruins,
as the throngs of death pass.

. . . .

They are far away with their sorrow
still warm beside the low church candles
where they revealed on their bent brows
life all joyous at the height of noon,
when spells and stars dwindle.

But night has no faith in the dawn,
and love lives to weave death,
just as the free soul,
a cistern teaching silence,
within the burning city.

TEFCROS ANTHIAS

1900–. Born in Cyprus. Lived for many years in Athens. His best known poetry is the collection titled as The Whistlings of the Vagabond. *Other works:* Serenades, Greece, The Human Epic *(translated into English by A. Raysson). Prose:* Living Cyprus.

THE CLOWN

Poor, lonely clown, somersaulting horribly,
here and there in the theatre of life,
you'll find yourself on some road like useless rubbish,
on a wintry night, an icy evening.

The dim light of day will have died . . . died,
and they will light no torches nor tapers for you.
Only your friends, the clowns, with hands crossed
and in flickering unison will chant: "Blameless on the way" . . .

What of it? You played your roles well
and they applauded you sincerely or in jest,
and "glory, glory be to God" you chuckled with
the loge, and the orchestra and the pit.

HANDS THRUST IN POCKETS

> *"Holy, holy, holy*
> *Lord of Sabbaoth,*
> *the sky and earth are full of Thy glory*
> *Hosannah! In the highest."*

Hands thrust in pockets, I look up quickly
at the clouding sky, cheating sky!
Surely God, the Almighty, is angry
with some blundering angel.

TEFCROS ANTHIAS

The north wind must be a fine doctor, no doubt,
making deadly injections in my body,
planing my bones and joints.
Almighty God! Am I a sinner?

I never stole—though I should have—
I never committed a crime, so called, usually caused
by the laws and customs of the day and age.
Why then, gracious Lord, do you punish me?

Haha! I laugh, I laugh like the very devil.
Do you really exist? Then destroy yourself,
since, Mighty Philanthropist, you are not shocked
seeing so many evils . . . from on high.

Two tramps are still shivering at the corner.
I approach them with respect and compassion.
Ah! the frost enfolds the three of us . . .
I want to shake my fists . . . but . . . I am cold.

EPILOGUE

Tramp! Tonight the night is so fine, so fine;
you may even sleep on a little bench, tramp.
Thought has broadened life so much, so much,
that man has made the earth and all the universe: a home.

You have no tears to mourn your lot, nor strength to endure it,
nor hysterical cries to shriek far and wide,
you are a silent wave of an unending storm
subsiding restlessly in the quiet dusk.

And when you find salvation sprawled there on a little bench,
and the whirlwind, the storm of your life grows calm,

tramp! you will never say you were tired
of the harsh struggle of your discordant soul.

Tramp! Tonight the night is so fine, so fine,
you may even sleep on a little bench, tramp.
Thought has broadened life so much, so much,
that man has made the earth and all the universe: a home.

JOSEPH ELIYIA

1901-1931. Born in Yanina. He was a teacher of French and Hebrew at the Alliance Francaise in Yanina. He wrote on all Hebrew subjects for the Large Encyclopedia, and his poems were published posthumously by the B'Nai B'rith to which he left his scattered poetry when he died suddenly in Athens. A book of his poems has been translated into English by Rae Dalven.

OUR TORAH

                    Dedicated to some slaves of the ghetto.
Day and night, steeped in sterile study,
with your pale features, ever withered by poverty,
within your cobwebbed obsolete Talmud—hunched,
your enslaved souls reseek with passion,
to find what our Torah writes.

But O blind, in your march of time,
in this ancient faded faith, have you not sensed
the archaic oil-lamp snuffed? A new light ahead on our road!
And life's quick unfolding no longer seeks
to find what our Torah writes.

Like a many mouthed hydra, the thick skinned Lord, O horror,
will suck you insatiate, in your divine condemnation,
while your slave soul, miserable crumb, shadow of a rag,
moulders each day. But he, know it, does not seek
to find what our Torah writes.

O brothers, bewitched by your ancient grandeur,
come, let us scan the living book of life,
there you will find something underscored

with the rod of the satrap and the chains of the worker,
horrible that our Torah does not write that!

JESUS

> "Nothing in the story of mankind is able to
> equalize the love which He inspired, the
> solace which He spread, the good which
> He engendered, the hope which He kindled
> in the breast of mankind."—*A Jewish View
> of Jesus*, Rabbi H. G. Enelow.

Tonight I also came, sweet brother of Nazareth,
drowning barbaric passion and savage hate within me,
to weep before the bleeding body of thy more beautiful
soul, that never in this world had flourished.

O modest lily of Galilee, towards thy white light,
how often fluttered the hope of the humble!
Numerous crosses arose opposite thine,
kin and strangers, Pharisees and Crucifiers.

Thou art neither the first nor the last crucified,
sweet Jesus, in this world of gall and hate,
but thy glory, immaculate in the race of mortals:
Whether or not the son of God,—Thou art the God of Pain!

MILITARISM

The black city is mute and as if in meditation,
vainly searching they say, for the happiness that passed;
a wraith-like form stalks by, in khaki;

lightning slides snake-like into my heart's gloom,
and in silent squares and in silent alleys,
"tran, tran," echo the spurs.

Within the soul re-echo the winds of carnage;
in her desolated house the old woman recalls her son;
a mother squeezes her babe in her embrace and shudders,
as a passerby sings: "The son of Psiloriti,"
And in silent squares and in silent alleys,
"tran, tran," echo the spurs.

The heart restrains its tear and chills again from terror,
thick darkness in the soul and the boots threaten,
some laborer with drooped shoulder blasphemes;
a hoarse dog barks—barks—
And in silent squares and in silent alleys,
"tran, tran," echo the spurs.

KASSARIS EMMANUEL

> *1902–. Born in Athens. His first collection of verse appeared in 1929. Works: Poems, Twelve Sullen Masks, Dynasty of Chimeras. Translations: Edgar Allen Poe, Valerie's Narcissus, Heredia's The Afternoon of a Faun, Igitur by Stephen Mallarmé.*

DYNASTY OF CHIMERAS

Heavily-laden, snow-white, she departed from the shadow and
The Ideal, wailing in her pompous crypt   [bitter flowers!
must have etherealized her lambent, lithe body
into myrrh for the bloody jubilees of the roses.

From a fathomless abyss that Absence has dug,
her star-studded memory dawns, moves to mid-sky and sets
in a melancholic waste of precious stones.

Poetry laments. On the funeral frieze
of her tomb bearing the shadow of her exquisite beauty, she
                              [has lost colors, symbols, myths.

5.

Skin, a glory of limpid, filagree gold!
Oh hair, boughs of golden fruit, hair where
the flaming bronzes of setting suns tremble!

The eyes—a musical Mediterranean sky—
there, its fine weather, joyful, with sapphire springs glows.
Over these the pale lightning of two vigorous arcs
support the melancholy sky of the forehead.
A slow dream woven in a ring of opium!

11.

Dissolved, a granite vision is created
for the long, frightful delusions of the senses.
When she loosens her hair, a starless night spreads
in polar skies of old-fashioned mirrors,
she gleams, a fiery flash of leaden desires,
dangerous as a ravine and alluring as sin.
It is not a creation of perishable, crystalline loves;
azure flame of a lyric frenzy:

Bronze sphinx, idol of black magic,
destined for the rigid idolatries of Asiatics,
for the doomed hysterical voodoos of the blacks.

15.

She blossomed in the silence of a very ancient monastery,
in the musical striking of crystalline matins.
While praying in secret before pale icons,
her saintly soul resembled a cracked old vase.

Her soul melted frankincense, mysteriously united
to a tender madonna and lovable lily.

At twilight, as a gold, meek light slid
towards the realm of shadows, the lily escaped.

Then its soul filled with sorrowful Ideal.
She resembled a dim, spectral cypress
and one night a stunned angel, gathering
the emerald of its soul in her luminous palm,
melted it into diaphanous dew-frozen stars.

THE HAUNTED SHIP

Here is this frail, phantom ship again!
Mute, as always, it glides through the dead waters tonight—
An ebon light giving birth to a misty shadow when
the storm vomited tar and sulphur in the chaos.

It started out of the ghostly horizon, beyond the deep.
At its stern, where death built its throne
a black flag, woven by dense storm clouds
unfurls its nightmare shadow.

The lighthouse keepers who live exiled in desolate towers
see this in the Erebus of wintry nights
sailing like a monster phantom, while a misty light
mournfully shines, like torn Hope, on her mast.

The archipelago breezes did not rock that boat
nor did the joyful cries of the albatross say
that under the sapphire tropical skies,
as the golden balsam sea-weeds fall,

the wave swoons like a voluptuous woman
in the rosy embrace of fragrant shores.
Her black sails dawned on dead seas
like last, nightmare thoughts of the dying.

Hypnotized by the opiate mists of the sly fog,
she sails blindly to monstrous lands,
where pale suns in ancient frozen orbits
shine on empty skies like fantastic flowers.

She saw mysterious islands of dark basalt
buried beneath the fiery rain of volcanoes,
and with a knell, as if countless underground bells tolled,
rolling in the dark depths and abysses of the sea.

In her passage she buried the fluting winds.
If something sighed bitterly on Acheron nights
it was not the wind: the pale souls of survivors
lament on the mournful harp of her masts.

This boat did not anchor in a peaceful harbor.
(Peace fled from it like a terrified halcyon)
A phantom of ages past, vagrant, an omen of secret depths
it saw indestructible suns, skies and seas fading.

And it sails and sails, this frail, phantom ship!
Its only comrades, trusted followers of its trips,
some skeleton birds always follow, always
a company of ever flying coffins.

MICHALIS STASINOPOULOS

> 1903—. Born in Callamata. Studied law and served in the Government Committee of the Agricultural and Aeronautical Bureau. He has published scientific works and helped compile the Large Encyclopedia. He is a contributor of poetry, articles and translations to various magazines.

CHESS KNIGHT

Cautious and still, mute and absorbed,
obedient to the black or white, fixed, deep in thought,
he suddenly leaps, taking a stand on the black or the white
and broods on the unsociable and speechless game:

One move, two moves, a thought, another thought.
His wooden foes surround him with their traitorous plans.
What strategy can he devise or plan?
Within the narrow squares, all thought is bounded.

And so his life is unvaried, has a sameness!
One move, two moves; one thought, the same thought!
He surveys and estimates the silent game.

For he knows that he for all his life is doomed
to rush amid his wooden foes and fall,
heroic, on the black or the white, beside his king!

THE YOUNG PROVINCIAL

You brought your childlike eyes to the capital,
and the buttons and gold braids of your college,
a fragrance of lemon trees locked in gardens,

and of flowers blooming in a monastary garden.
You also brought a timid little soul, injured
by angles of the compass and standard measuring rods.
Now, tell me, where will you go in your tightly buttoned [uniform,
to present this little soul so mathematical?
Now you fear to look through doors ajar
that may conceal a hidden promise in their shade.
You still fear (and your black eyes mist over)
lest people jest and laugh at your untutored soul.
But I know this: some rosy hour of summer,
passing outside this door ajar and incredulous,
I will see cast over the old worn steps
(like someone's corpse slain in the dark)
a gold-braided, child's chiton.

SOPHIA MAVROIDI PAPADAKY

1905–. Born in Crete. She studied at the Faculty of Letters of Athens and became a high school teacher of modern Greek Literature. Her first collection of verse: Hours of Love *(1934).* Verse of Youth and Liberty *won for her the poetry prize of Resistance. In prose she has written:* The Tale of Olympos *(1941),* 22 Tales for Youth *and* Two Tales for Children. *She has translated into Greek, Galsworthy's* The Property Owner, Rebecca *by Daphne du Maurier, and the French novel by Elsa Triolet,* No One Loves Me. *A large part of her original work, translations and critical articles are scattered in various literary reviews to which she has been contributing for the last 20 years.*

TO A MOTHER

Little son whom I lift with the wings of my dream
to fairy-land, to places of song;
for you I tremble lest my word or deed
blur your eye or check your wish . . .
So many whirlwinds, so many lightnings and rains,
so many rapiers sharpened by hate,
on the crossroads in ambush for you!

My little son whom I cover with the mantle of my care,
an indrawn breath from you makes me grow pale.
How many coming evils, dangers and diseases
set up their nets to enmesh you!

My little son, in your children's games
I never let the tools of war inflame your soul.
I pasture your desires in gardens of love,
and I launch your cravings from waveless harbors.

With what herbs and charms can I subdue the monster,
for as long as mountains stand and mothers give birth,
never to put the bow of hatred
and the banner of slaughter in the hand of man!
My little son, would that I might live as long as you,
a thousand ply shield guarding you from ill.

THE LITTLE SERVANT

A frail little body,
her braids a wreath
on her little head.
How I remember Lenio!
A little servant in a house
where I was a governess.

Of about the same age,
capricious, spoiled—
a little lady—
my pupil Lucia
tormented me
and poor Lenio.

How I recall the longing
in the little servant's
two large eyes,
each a question mark,
as she came with the tray
to serve the governess.

She pretended to be tidying,
when she was in the room,
always pricking up her ear,

always standing near the desk,
she would stare at the book.

And for her sake I spoke
with passion and fire.
And I'd begin to tell a story
about Nereids, spirits,
about crystalline palaces.
And the little one, lost in thought,
would drink me in with her eyes.

Till a voice came from the side
as if out of the fairy-tale
an angry gorgon
had dispelled the magic from us
and saddened, the little servant
returned to the kitchen.

With her large eyes
each a question mark
what became of Lenio?
What became of the poor child?
She must be a servant in some other house
just as I am a poor governess,
in another house.

ALTAR OF LIBERTY

This is a grove where the leaves of the trees
are woven into nightingales' nests,
from time to time, a shudder of death
convulses it just before dawn.

Deep dawn! A silent company,
gallant bodies bound in chains,

rudely awakened from sleep
walk on their last march.

Valiant men, whose only sin
was liberty's flame leaping within,
the light shed by their blameless steps
and justice their secret passion.

Gentle dawn, take fragrance from their soul
and light from their brilliant brows
and strew your purple roses for them
make your misty shawl their shroud.

The gruesome salvo of guns
barbarously stirred the silence
the whole neighborhood is shaken from sleep
and oh, it knows the meaning . . . and sighs.

In a little while, in a wagon
piled hastily one over the other,
the heroic bodies pass,
bathed for death by the dawning light.

And at daybreak, each passerby
perceived with misty eye
a purple line of drops of blood
adorning the narrow lane.

Brothers, this narrow lane traced
by your pure blood, will broaden,
will shine a gigantic avenue
from sunrise to sundown,

till there is enough room for the throngs
of tyrannized slaves
to go toward the light to rest
at last from their slavery redeemed.

LOVE SONG

What is this thing that keeps me tirelessly waiting
        hours till you go by?
As if my heart were breaking, and I feel I turn pale
        when they mention your name?
Why should your shadow alone fill the world,
        you have but to appear
and I feel the wave of life seething
        ceaselessly within me!
Why should I lower my eyes beneath the glance
        I crave so much,
forget, when you spoke, the answer
        I had planned for days?
What is this thing assuming the guise of first love
        that comes at such a time?
A brilliant sun that, I know, always drags lightning behind,
        a downpour of rain?
If it is the last message of youth, I await it,
        I welcome it a thousand times
A triumphant twilight, sent by the light,
        before the night fades.

NICHOLAS PAPPAS

1906—. Born in Trikkala, Thessaly. Studied in Athens and is now a practicing lawyer. He edited The Province *(1931-32). Poetical works:* Vain Words *(1943),* Captive Angels *(1945),* A Four-Year Night *(1947),* The Fairy-Tale of the Sleep-Walker *(1948). He has written treatises and articles in newspapers and magazines.*

POST-WAR ROLL CALL

Those nights with the glorious woes are over.
Come now, let us be counted,
to learn which of our brothers are missing,
to look into each other's eyes with great love,
to look deeply into ourselves,
as if we had suddenly become acquainted,
to talk about the little children who have died,
to recall unknown villages destroyed
that we loved like our own native land,
to listen through tears of joy
to the dirges that shrouded us
when they hanged the children on our ancestral squares,
to hear the story of black robed mothers,
to count our life—drop by drop,
the terror we suffered
among the shadows locked in the house.

Come, let us see who have forgotten us,
how many remain in strange valleys
to grow the grass tall with their young bodies,
to pave the road of resistance with resolute bodies.
Our homes have caught fire and who will put them out?

Our forests and crops are on fire.
The peasant cannot find his hut in his village;
the shepherd cannot find his flocks,
our city streets have changed;
our mansions have again become boulders.

We are not human beings, we have no heart.
Within us resides a huge beast;
we shiver outside of the alien warmth
among the ruins the cave-dwellers freeze.

Come. Let us see how many the war has branded for us.
Come. Let us look deep into each other's eyes.
Perhaps we may find again the warm heart;
perhaps once more we may see the children
who started from the camp of the foe
to return to their village . . .
Carry plenty of water from the mountain springs
to wash our hands well—
our hands dyed in blood.
Your child's locks have grown long;
you kept leaving him behind and he kept growing,
his brow has hardened uncaressed;
he ate grass on the ground while you advanced,
while you raised banners in foreign countries
to strengthen the master who tyrannized over you
to grasp the bread from pale children
reared as their own by neighbors.
They burned the houses that warmed us,
they hanged our brothers on wild trees,
the meadows have remained orphan.
Why? Why, my comrades?
Our houses that waited for us with doors ajar,
the old people greeting us each morning at the corner,
we who loved the free wind . . .

We have all become ashes and a bitter dream . . .
Why? Why, my comrades?

FOUR YEARS

Four years passed and all of us did not die.
We lived for four years under criminal orders;
we saw boys disfigured in blood,
trucks with bodies that mothers rummaged;
we heard unlawful knocks on our door;
we saw Germans pick those who were to die,
we imagined unconquered ships weighing anchor,
decked in flowers, festive.

Consider the boys who died before squads,
intoxicated by their fourteen years,
a great temple in their hearts,
with large hands that clasped the hands of all peoples;
a magic fruit in their palms
which they cast behind them as they were being killed;
and these large fields blossomed,
filled with flags and signals,
flooded with colors of such rapture.
Consider the boys who guarded the crossroads,
in France, in Athens, in Oslo,
with rifle on their breasts,
breathing heavy odours
of hatred and vengeance.
They stayed in occupied cities, young and beardless.
Laughing they played with death.
They held the suburbs and neighborhoods of the capital
and when foreign soldiers trembled before their shadow,
they held our soul high on the mast of hope,

Greece and our proud people,
with the triumphant feelings of youth.

Dark night shrouded all of Europe,
Prussian peasants patrolled our villages,
our breaths were concealed in icy rooms,
my two brothers were away on the mountains;
distant aeroplanes droned like bees,
the aeroplanes of our free friends;
our hearts opened like a message,
glances gleamed in the night;
stealthily, as in fairy-stories, we raised the window,
in the distance we saw the gleam of their arrival
and we sent them our enslaved greetings
gently, so they might return . . .
Four years they kept betraying us and murdering us.
Four years we were resisting and defeating them.
Clandestinely we whispered profound words.
Glorious hands distributed secret newspapers.
Secret eyes signalled to us,
the night when death kept vigil on the streets,
boys shivering on the back streets of the capital,
marking the national colors on the walls
with fearful scarlet letters
that would have heralded its will of dawn.
Four years. Each day we might have died.
They told us they burnt our house.
They told us they shot our little brother.
The boys of the neighborhood were lost to concentration
Ah, won't we ever see each other again?   [camps.
Will we see again the little girl
girdled with belt of leaden weapons;
her little body on indomitable sentinel
guarding a great avenue?

NICHOLAS PAPPAS

Each day in the communities they picked boys.
How many of us will be left?
We are like phantoms of fine metal.
The Germans have reached the Volga and the Nile.
No one believes they will conquer us.
No one unbuckles his arms.
The wind carries underground messages to us,
the mountains are filled with wrath and Greeks.
When did the four years pass?
We used to say good morning like conspirators.
Let us be careful not to forget our dead.
Four years passed, let us not forget each other.
Liberty is deeply hidden.
Its martyrs are great.
Let us be careful not to forget our beardless boys.
Four years and they did not let us die.
A night of four years for us to sleep . . .

RITA BOUMY PAPPAS

1906–. Born in Syra. She grew up and studied in Sicily. She returned to Greece in 1930 and published her first book Songs to Love *in 1935. The* Pulse of Silence *received the Academy Award.* Athens, December 1944 *appeared in 1945, and* The New Grass *in 1949. She edited the magazine* Cyclads *for years, and has also done translations from the French and Italian.*

ATHENS (excerpts)

Athens is critically ill.
A few hours ago she threw off her head band.
In spite of her burning fever she struck the drums of revolt.
Disheveled, breast open like a statue of madness
clad in freedom from top to toe
she paces through the historic December fog.

Athens sounded the alarm at midnight,
with bells, sirens, she said, 'No,'
with a guitar of Pheraios,
with sticks, arms and flaming firewood.
The horses coming from the stable neigh with her;
the hounds that sniffed out a new stranger;
the hungry children who angrily threw away
the bread of alms
sated with the milk of their country.

. . . .

The bishops abandoned the churches,
the students their school benches,
the gypsies their tents,
and all rally to you, their hands burning pikes.

RITA BOUMY PAPPAS

All the laurels of Ilyssos were plucked,
rugged Eurotas sent its own,
the laurels drown Athens in a green rain.

Hairless, male chests stone cold,
dead boys and girls who never finished their lessons,
boys with two syllable honeyed names,
glory seized them and left beyond the sea.

. . . .

Freedom, you fed our children with opium,
here in the city canopied by faithless clouds,
opium and the girl holding the gun like a sceptre,
gleaming as no statue could gleam in this city
as her flaxen hair poured out of the helmet.
We saw you, we saw you unkissed girls,
your armored stature was not a dream!

. . . .

How they love freedom on this soil!
A great vulcan burst in your breast.
In the heart of the world's winter
the pariahs of earth will come to warm themselves in your fire,
star of the new December.

. . . .

Athens, Athens, city of the great sun
there is no room for night in your Parthenon.
They cannot comprehend your wealth
for they have never worn a vestment of splendor,
or sandals from the panoply of Achilles,
they did not drink almond milk before the sun hardened it.

YIANNIS SPHAKIANAKIS

1907–. Born in Crete. Prose works: Short Stories *(1932),* Centaurs *(drama 1935),* Uncreative Nights *(short stories, 1936),* Agnes Polyla *(novel, 1943),* The Leaders of the Shadows of the Aegean *(novel). Critical Studies:* Introduction to Lyric Myth *(1939),* Thought and Poetry in Neohellenic Years *(1940),* A Man from the House of Acacias *(1941). Translations:* Prose-Poems: Rimbaud, Requiem *by Rainer Maria Rilke, published in Nea Estia 1938,* Letters to a Young Poet *by Rilke published in Neo-Hellenic letters, 1939. Poetical works include:* Last Poems *(1937),* The Myth of Drops *(1938),* Traveling Isles *(1941).*

THE SONG OF FREEDOM AND THE SEA

I toss my black hair
like the crest of our Eagle
and I fly where your wound calls me
From the depths of the valley of God,
all is freedom in the field
all is freedom in the sea
all is joy at the source of our life.

I kneel at your wound
that stays open
to receive the seed of my plea
I come with our white horse
and I brought freedom over the sea
crossing the source of your tears
a source open to the wind
to receive the plea of the infinite.

Dress yourself too
my little sister Agnes
in the flesh of people
and come through the fields of sun
with the sorrowful women of the earth
to the house I have built for you
at the edge of the sea.

YIANNIS RITSOS

1909—. Born in Nonemvasie. Attended high school in Gytheio, then came to Athens where he has lived ever since. His books are: Crater *(1934),* Pyramids *(1935),* Epitaph *(1936),* The Song of My Sister *(1937),* Spring Symphony *(1938),* The March of the Ocean *(1940),* Old Mazourka, In the Rhythm of the Rain *(1943),* Trial *(1945),* Our Comrade *(1945).*

TO MY SISTER (excerpt)

My sister
only you
are left me
to lean on your heart
and listen to the pulse
of men.
Behind the vaults
of your eyes
my life journeys.
You came affectionately on tip-toe
on nights when sad and silent
I wrote furious verses
about clamorous wars
of fire
and blood.
I surmised your presence
back of the night.
The honeysuckle fragrance
of tender hours
filled my ash covered roof
as soon as your step
was heard.

With your smile
the whole sky entered
my room.
Sweet changing shadows
danced on the walls
and the memory of the country
rippled under my touch.
When I returned, bent
from my night wanderings
and from the proud bitterness
of my solitude,
I found the loving dinner
steaming on the table
and the memory of our childhood
played like a delicate moth
around your lamp.
You stayed awake
awaiting my return.
And when I,
lover of the infinite,
plunged into shadows
and ether of doubt
you
with a kind finger
pointed out to me the earth's paths,
remoulded my ashes
into human shape.
I shared
your chair
and thus I kept
a seat on earth.
My pulse beat time
with yours.
Somewhere near me I heard

drops of water falling
from a hidden spring
and the spring died.
You went away.
You took with you
the heaven of yourself
behind your footsteps.
The snow is falling.
Ah Life! Life!
You have taken from me
the last morsel of flesh.
I have no more tears.
I have no fear.
I have nothing else they can take from me.
Destitute, naked and all alone!
See my wealth
that no one can
take from me.
I will knock at no door.
I will ask no alms.
Without bread,
without a wallet,
without a ring,
I take the road to the west
with wide, steady strides,
naked but entire
worthy to come close to God.

SPRING SYMPHONY (excerpt)

You pace
through my dusty rooms
in wide spring dress

fragrant of green leaves,
freshly washed sky
and sea-gull wings
over a morning sea.

Within your eyes echo
some small tunes of
harmonicas played by
the happiest children
in vernal country places.

Look at the photographs—
the dead mother,
the dead brother,
and my pale little sisters
with curls like moons
and a far-away smile
suspended on their faces,
like a cage of canaries
hanging in a wretched house
where all have died.

Where is a porter
to move this household stuff
to the cellar?

Holding hands
we will walk down the wooden staircase
worn out by the footsteps
of autumnal shadows.

Let us go to the fields
to wear on our fingers
the poppies and the sun.

See the running sun
in the woods.

We are not late.

. . .

The carillons of light
welcomes us
at the yellow seashore.
The dawn crosses the beach
barely wetting her bare heels
in the gold-tipped wave.

A young girl
opened the window,
smiled at the sea
and shut her eyes to the light
to contemplate profoundly
the dull gleam
of her own smile.

Hear the carillons
of the country churches!

They come from afar
from the heights.
From the lips of children
from the ignorance of swallows
from the white courts of Sunday
from the honeysuckle and the dovecotes
of the humble houses.

Listen to the carillons
of the spring churches.

. . .

I shut my eyelids
beneath the placid night
and I hear ten thousand stars singing
where your fingers crept
on my flesh.

I see the starry summer sky.
I have grown so profound,
so beautiful, so big
through your love
that you can no longer embrace me.

Dearest, let us share
the gifts you brought me.
See, the forest sags
from the weight of its flowers.

NICEPHORUS VRETTAKOS

1911—. Born in Levetsova, Sparta. Attended high school in Gytheon, a port in the southern Peloponnese. Since 1930 he has been living in Athens where the following books of his verse have been published: Descending to the Silence of the Centuries *(1933),* Grimaces of Man *(1935),* The War *(1935),* The Letter of the Swan *(1937),* The Voyage of the Archangel *(1938),* Margarita *(1939),* The Peak of the Fire *(1940),* The Heroic Symphony *(1944),* 33 Days *(1945),* Fairy Tale City *(1947). His prose works include:* The Naked Child *(1939),* The Savage *(1945). Vrettakos won the Government Prize for 1940.*

CHILD OF THE WIND WITH THE HARMONICA

No longer will the machine gun decide for liberty.
No longer will tormenters suppress us.
No longer will they come out to face you,
child of the wind with the harmonica!
Sidewalk statue blown by the mistral,
standing on one foot, piping your nation's sorrows,
with a brook-like voice, singing from your heart,
tiny heart of liberty quivering like the morning-star,
child of the wind with the harmonica!

The pepper trees of the avenue became part of your blood.
Your blood was a bird that flew on high and sang to us
higher than the cypresses of Constitution Square!
Titiv, titsiou! Don't be afraid! Titiv, titsiou! Don't be afraid.
You were the bird and the almond tree, the star and the
outlined by the lightning flashed on our door   [window
that was embraced by death at night to force it open.

NICEPHORUS VRETTAKOS

Naked, you pushed back the darkness! And we, what can we
 [say to you!
Our heart cannot bear the dizzy heights of your greatness,
child of the wind with the harmonica!

Tell us, poet of poets, how we may sing your praises!
Comrade of our hope, tell us what to name you.
Tell us because our lips suffer!
We do not want our words to fall on the ground!
We do not want to fail in such a task!
Else, rather we had come out to be killed in battle!
Else, rather we had sailed with the ships at sea,
than steal the bread crumbs of the hopeless
while you guard alone the narrow passes of night,
purer than Christ's love
for the daisies of the field
child of the wind with the harmonica!

I will go out to the field to gather the fallen leaves of the sun,
to transform its rays—this summer—
to transform its rays into pages, to record
the sky and your song, Greek boy!
Because the soil is not enough! My blood is not enough!
Because my tears are not enough to mould my clay!
What good is my house! Outdoors they sing your praises!
Outdoors they speak of you! My voice is not enough!
I will run where I heard you say 'No' to death!
I will run where you used to go piping in defiance
of the thunderbolt! Defying commands and the sweet bread
defying your own blue eyes created for love!   [of the earth,

And I will shake down your sorrowful tunes from the pepper-
 [trees!
And I will gather your little notes! And I will cover the Holy
of my poetry with your sackcloth shirt;   [Altar

and I will gather the wild flowers as though I raise your flag
to plant it at my country's entrance,
at the entrance of time and ships. As though I were raising
the Host of Greece from the asphalt,
riddled with holes by the foe's bullets! I will raise you
and set you with your harmonica on a bronze base,
standing on one foot, leaning your shoulder careless,
beneath the little clouds of time
in the center of Constitution Square!
How shall I conceive you, name you, paint you!
Child of the wind with the harmonica!

ELEGY ON THE GRAVE OF A SMALL FIGHTER

Over your grave we pronounce our name.
Over your grave we plan our gardens and cities.
Over your grave we Are. We have a nation.

I have cherished your gun-shot within me,
the poisonous stutter of the machine gun echoes within me,
I remember your heart that was rent, and to my mind come
some hundred petaled roses
like the speech of the Infinite to man.
Thus your heart spoke to us.
And we saw that the world is greater,
and it became wider so love might have a place.
Your first little toy was you.
Your first little horse was you.
You played the role of fire. You played the role of Christ.
You played the roles of St. George and Digenis.
You played the hands of the watch descending from midnight.
You played the voice of hope where there was no voice.
The square was deserted. Our nationhood had gone.

The time had come! Your heart could bear it no longer—
to hear the human thunder of Europe under your roof!
Under your little jacket, you lit your first dark lantern,
heart of hearts! You thought of the sun and you advanced.

You climbed to the sidewalk and you played the man!

ATHENS

Athens. It is midnight.
The candles weep in the City of Cities!
Athens. It is midnight.

Gigantic square tower
set on the brow of the planet,
garden city of stars, of glory illumined by sun,
of virtue on your unique crest,
where golden eagles meet from east and west,
where people clasp hands tempest-tossed by great passion,
where you gleam lit by the barbed wire on your brow,
gallows, black clouds, death. Ah, you, on
the Zalongo of history, dance singing
the slogans of the age in the universal night!

Each rag on your starving children
makes the world hold you in greater esteem.

In their pride your heroes sigh so faintly
that none may hear but Liberty
who like a mother now gives all one pillow for their heads,
covering them all with her star-filled mantle
on sidewalks, in prisons, in camps . . .

Athens! Athens!
Your blood sinks to earth's heart. Trees tremble.

Mercenaries strike at you. The sun enfolds you.
Glorious swords point you out. The free people
of the earth, heads bared, weep as they gaze at you.
Flame! Pillar! Guerrilla Girl! The clouds
of your fire light the whole world!

Athens! It is midnight.
Candles weep in the City of Cities.
Athens. It is midnight.

JUST ONE MORE SPRING

Comrades, I say this not to make you sad,
not to make you sit on the stones and grieve.
Take out the horse, saddle it and let the captain mount!

Just one more spring . . . one more summer,
just one more spring . . . enslaved, enslaved . . .

Do not be lulled to sleep by your sorrow.
New clouds hover over our nation!
Black masses of clouds hang like leaden weights
over us, our houses, the graves of our children!
The sun becomes a red moon; our mountains
put on their gray knapsacks in formation,
and a bitter echo rises out of ravines—
something like the roar of the sea pronged by sorrow,
something like the mother's bitter moan looking sadly at the
and musing on love in the world. [sun

Here in this land so strange where the rivers,
the very stones and gorges, the clouds and the mountains
come forth to fight for us and they battle and are wounded,
here on these trees where guerrillas and klephts have floated,
—Byron is dead! Byron died a long time ago,   [their songs,

and since he left not a single descendent for his Greece,
what have the soldiers of his land come to do here today
that we can tell the birds to sing to him?

We waited for them to come to make new offerings to us—
a few flowers from the earth of our beloved Shelley.
And they came to crucify our people, our Adonis,
our Adonis with a thousand wounds! Awake,
let us seize in our hands our country's trumpets!

Let us make them understand: Olympos cannot be razed!
Let us make them understand that the sun has not changed,
that the colors never change in this land
and that the song of freedom has never been broken.
When the 'old man of Morea' leaves off, Ares takes it up again,
when the young klephts leave off the men of ELAS take it up,
the high peaks take it, the rivers lead it on,
the seas break it in foam, the lairs blaze with it,
Morea and Roumely!

Just one more spring . . . one more summer,
just one more spring . . . enslaved, enslaved . . .

33 DAYS (the winter of 1944-45—excerpts)

Thus it happened then in Greece.

In those days a strong wind blew from the west.
And clouds came out of the north and rose to the horizon,
and you could not see the sunrise,
and strange currents that seemed to come from the south
and from the east and from the north furrowed the clouds.
And every day the crowd grew in numbers and they huddled
in the squares and they spilled over onto the sidewalks
and they beat their breasts and the city heard the moan

of their wave and it feared the Lord, and it felt sorrow
and sighed.

And on the third day of December, the Supreme Law—the
divine law and the human law which meet on Mount Sinai
and take the shape of a thunderbolt
and make the Nations quake
began to sound its heroic symphony over the city.

And on that day, brief disturbing signs crowded against
each other under the clouds.
And the forest swayed against the wind.
And the people advanced.
And the ambush waited.
And the people advanced against them, strong and beautiful
and conscious of right, like Christ.
And the people stretched out their palms to block the
muzzles of the guns that suddenly appeared shining against
their breasts.
And the volleys struck the holy temple of the State.
And the wounded dipped the flags in their blood and rising
on their swaying knees lifted them higher.
And some fell prone on the asphalt.
And others dragged them to the edges of the street chanting,
"Liberty and Justice!"
And they lay supine one after the other and each wrapped
himself in his blood-stained flag and clenched his fist
on his chest and died.

Thus it happened then in Greece.

Then wearing their helmets, our soldiers began to march
down, in close formation, to the center of the city.
And our soldiers were handsome like the Achaeans.

And we asked them about their horses; and they smiled.

They had their horses and armies within them.
And within them they had scarlet horses that glistened and neighed and leaped
And the horsemen sat on golden saddles.
And they wore gleaming jackets, golden jackets and light with sun.
Because it was the sun of liberty that carried them in his train.

Thus it happened then in Greece.

And bullets criss-crossed that night lighting the windowpanes of the city.
And through the city streets, desolation walked hand in hand with death.
And the last proclamation of the army commander went unnoticed on the walls.
The girls were carrying bullets.
The old women were singing.
And our soldiers were fighting without food or sleep.
And the "Lord Byron" student battalion, fighting in the center of the city recited verses from the "Curse of Athena" and wondered what could console the shade of Byron in this world. And Elgin answered guffawing as he sat on the heavy cannons that furrowed the dark with the course of their shells.
And with each of their volleys the Acropolis was lit.
And in their gleam at the very top you could see the Temple quaking.
And fighting they visioned endless orchards and new cities and churches and new bells and . . .
Christ is risen!
Christ is risen!
And they fought with a smile.
And the stretchers cut through the songs on the streets.

And the nurses erect amid the bullets lowered their white blood-stained flags and wiped their eyes.

"Liberty or death!"

Thus it happened then in Greece.

And the roaring cannons searched out our soldiers fighting without food and without sleep.
And with each of their volleys light and rain poured on our window panes and out on the street Christ was walking all alone.
And every now and then, as he faced the blazing muzzles of the cannons, Christ would open his mouth, like a bird, without food and without sleep.

And the barricades grew higher.

And the women tore their petticoats to bandage the wounded.
And while dying our soldiers still stood straight upon the barricades.
And the women would come out at the windows and see the night blend with the day and they would wipe their eyes.
"In the harbours, my children, they are unloading cannons and tanks."
And our soldiers turned their heads and smiled under their helmets and answered them by taking aim.

And our soldiers could still be heard singing in the darkness.
And the people's jailers rejoiced in their victory.
And they beat the air and the people with their whips.
And the water in broken pipes seethed mournfully in the chaos of the houses in ruins.
And the guards lashed the dead.

And on that night we took our pickaxes and we dug up the Attica earth and with many tears we buried our dead.

And the guards unburied them.
Then our women would get up at midnight and disperse in the dark.
And walking they hid in corners of buildings and at the roots of trees.
And once there they would return carrying the corpses of our boys in their arms.
And they would go down and wall up the basement windows and dig pits and bury them in their basements.
And they would go down there at night and light candles for them and throw flowers over them.

And they would gather in groups of five and ten
and kneel around them and sing the songs of
our gallant boys, as they wept: "You fought for five years."
And they would stand up and turn their heads to the sky looking for God, and they beat at their breasts.
"You fought for five years . . ."
And they would fall over the graves.
And their black hair reached down to hell.

And over the snow the flags of our soldiers retreated in formation.

Thus it happened then in Greece.

And Liberty knocked on the doors.
And they tried to chase her out of her own land.

And that night Byron was sighing as he sat high up on the Acropolis over the Saronic Gulf facing England.
And that night Sophocles awakened and Pindar and Solon and Plato.
And they wore the helmets of our dead.

And there appeared squadrons of French soldiers who had
been killed fighting in front of the Bastille.
Russian soldiers who had been killed in snow-covered
Petrograd.
Soldiers who had fallen in the university city of Madrid.
Women who had leaped over the cliffs of Zalongo.
And all of them had formed a circle high up on the
Acropolis.
And they paid homage.
And they presented arms as they looked at the sun and
saw in its flame the "Lord Byron" student battalion
marching past.

We fought for five years; and we are still fighting. And
in the prisons they made us wear the thorny wreath of
Christ, and they still make us wear it.

But over the mud where the mercenaries of night walk with
their whips, higher than all the prisons, higher, much
higher, higher than ever before, you can hear:
"Glory and honor to our dead! Glory and honor to our dead!"
Brothers of the world,
our flag is still waving.

"Liberty or death!"

ODYSSEUS ELYTIS

1912–. Pseudonym for Odysseus Alepoudelis. Born in Crete. Attended school in Athens, studied law at the University of Athens. He is strongly attracted to the surrealist movement and has written many articles on surrealism. In 1941-42 Elytis was a lieutenant in the Albanian campaign against the Italians. After the liberation Elytis published his long Lament for the Missing Lieutenant of the Albanian Campaign. *Two volumes of his verse have been published in Athens:* Orientations *(1941),* Sun the First *(1943).*

THE MAD POMEGRANATE TREE

In these pure white yards where the south wind blows
soughing through dim arcades, tell me is it the mad pome-
                                                                   [granate
trembling in the light, scattering the fruits of her laughter
in murmurs and wind stubbornnesses, tell me is it the mad
wriggling with foliage newly born in the dawn   [pomegranate
hoisting on high all colors in a triumphant tremor?

When naked girls waken in the plains,
mowing the clovers with their blonde hands
twisting the ends of their dreams, tell me is it the mad
                                                                     [pomegranate
that unsuspecting slips the lights in their green baskets,
flooding their names with song, tell me, is it the mad pome-
battling against the clouds of the world?   [granate

The day her jealousy adorned her with seven kinds of feathers
belting the eternal sun with a thousand prisms
dazzling, tell me is it the mad pomegranate

seizing the mane with a hundred lashes at full speed,
never sad, never cross, tell me is it the mad pomegranate
that cries out the new hope of dawning?

Tell me, is it the mad pomegranate offering greetings yonder,
shaking a handkerchief of leaves made of fresh flames,
a sea about to be born with a thousand and two boats
with waves that start and go a thousand and two times,
towards unexplored shores, tell me, is it the mad pomegranate
creaking the rigging on high, in the diaphanous air?

With the glaucus grapes high up in flames and feasting
haughty, full of perils, tell me, is it the mad pomegranate
breaking in light the demon's evils in the middle of the world,
spreading the saffron necklace of day to the horizon
richly embroidered, sown in song, tell me is it the mad pome-
quickly unhooking the silk of day? .   [granate

In April first's petticoats and the grasshoppers of August
                                          [fifteenth
tell me she who plays, she who is in a rage, who charms,
shaking the menace from her sad darkness,
pouring the drunken birds from the sun's armpits,
tell me she who spans her wings on the breast of things,
on the breast of our profound dreams, is it the mad pome-
                                                [granate?

HELEN

With the first drop of rain, the summer was killed.
The words that gave birth to star-beams were drenched,
all the words whose only destination was You!
Wherever we stretch our hands now that time no longer
                                                [considers us,

ODYSSEUS ELYTIS

wherever we let our eyes wander now that distant lines have
                                        [sunk in the clouds
now that your eyelids closed on our landscape,
we live—as if the fog passed through us—
alone, all alone, surrounded by your dead images.

With brow against the window pane we watch the new
it is not death will cast me down as long as you are, [sorrow,
as long as elsewhere a wind exists to play entirely of you,
dressing you near as our hope dresses you afar,
as long as elsewhere there is a verdant prairie beyond your
                                      [laughter up to the sun,
telling him in confidence that we will meet once more.
No, it is not death we will confront but a tiny drop of an
a confused feeling,   [autumnal rain,
the odour of the moist soil in our souls fading in time.

Even if your hand is not in mine,
even if my blood does not run in the veins of your dreams,
nor the light in the immaculate sky
nor even the unseen music inside me, O melancholy
passerby, the things that hold me to this world
are the humid air, the autumn hour, the separation,
the bitter support of the elbow on memory
surging when the night starts to separate us from the light
behind the square window that looks towards sadness
and sees nothing
for it is already become an invisible music, a flame in the
a carillon of the large clock on the wall   [chimney,
for it is already become
a poem, verse after verse, echo paralleling the rain, tears and
                                                [words,
words not like the others, but they too with their only destina-
                                                   [tion: You!

MARINA OF THE ROCKS

You have a taste of storm on your lips—but where did you [roam
all day long the hard dream of stone and sea?
The eagle-carrying wind has stripped the hills
stripped your desire down to the bone
and the pupils of your eyes took Chimera's baton
tracing the memory with foam!
Where is the familiar ascent of the short September
among the red clay where you played seeing at your feet
the deep bouquets of the other young girls,
the corners where your companions abandoned armsful of
[rosemary?
But where did you roam all night the hard dream of stone
[and the sea?
I entreated you to count its luminous days in the unclothed
to enjoy supine the dawn of things   [water
or roam again the yellow fields
a trefoil of light on your breast, iambic heroine.
You have a taste of storm on your lips
and a red, blood-like dress
deep in the summer gold
and the fragrance of hyacinths—but where did you roam
as you descended shorewards the pebbly gulfs?
Down there was a cold briny sea-weed
and further down a human feeling that bled.
Astonished you opened your arms pronouncing his name
as you lightly climbed to the limpid deep
where your own star-fish shone.

Listen, the word is the wisdom of the last
and time is an impassioned sculptor of men
and the sun stands over him, beast of hope

and closer to it, you hug a love with a bitter taste of storm
[on your lips.
You need not count, azure to the bone, on another summer
for rivers to change their current and carry you back to their
for you to kiss once more other cherry trees   [mother,
or ride on horseback in the mistral.

Pillared on the rocks without a yesterday or tomorrow
on the perils of rocks with the combing of the storm,
you will give final greeting to your enigma.

BIBLIOGRAPHY OF WORKS CONSULTED

IN GREEK:

The Lyre, Andreas Calvos. Geneva, 1824
Kyra Phrosini, Aristotelis Valaoritis. Corfu, 1859
Poems, Aristotelis Valaoritis. Athens, 1891
Poems, Dionysios Solomos. Athens, 1898
DIONYSIOS. Athens, October, 1901
260 Demotic Songs, George Pachtikos. Athens, 1905
Demotic Songs, Ayis Theros. Athens
Poems, Julius Typaldos. Athens, 1916
Poems, Yiannis Vilaras. Athens, 1916
Poems, Georgios Vizinos. Athens, 1916
LIFE. a literary magazine. Constantinople, 1920
The Altars, Kostes Palamas. Athens
The City and Solitude, Kostes Palamas. Athens
The Twelve Songs of the Gypsy, Kostes Palamas. Athens, 1921
Erotokritos, Vincenzo Kornaros. Athens
History of Neohellenic Literature, Elias Voutierides. Athens, 1924
The Immovable Life, Kostes Palamas. Athens, 1926
Slaves Besieged, Kostas Varnalis. Athens, 1927
Neohellenic Muse, A. Argyropoulos. Athens, 1928
Verses Mild and Harsh, Kostes Palamas. Chicago, 1928
Neohellenic Political History, Yiannis Kordatos. Athens
Daedalus in Crete, Angelos Sikelianos. Athens
Anthology of Greek Poems, Flamma. Athens, 1931
THE CYCLE. Athens, 1932
The Poet Cavafis, Timos Malanou. Nea Estia, June 15, 1933
Magic Refrains, Apostolos Melachrinos. Athens, 1934
Demotic Songs, Apostolos Melachrinos. Athens, 1935

WORKS CONSULTED

The Grave, Kostes Palamas. Athens, 1935
History of Neohellenic Literature, Aristes Kambanes. Athens, 1935.
Poems, C. P. Cavafy. Alexandria, Egypt, 1935
Our Songs, Yiannis Apostolakis. Athens, 1934
Apollonius, Apostolos Melachrinos, THE CYCLE. Athens, 1938
Anthology of Greek Poems (1738-1938), Heracles Apostolidi. Athens, 1938
Poems, Joseph Eliyia, B'nai Brith, Salonika, 1938
Odyssey, Nikos Kazantzakis. Athens, 1938
THE CYCLE. Athens, 1940
Traveling Isles, Yiannis Sphakianakis. Athens, 1940
Dynasty of Chimeras, Kassaris Emmanuel. Athens, 1940
Digenis Akritas, Henri Gregoire. New York, 1942
33 Days, Nicephorus Vrettakos. Athens, 1945
The Fairy-Tale City, Nicephorus Vrettakos. Athens, 1945
Poems, Odysseus Elytis. Athens, 1945
Poems, Georgios Seferis. Athens, 1945
Elefthera Grammata. 1945
The True Palamas, Nick Zachariades. New York, 1945
Poems of Youth and Liberty, Sophia Mavroidi Papadaky. Athens, 1946
Whistlings of the Tramp. Tefcros Anthias. Athens
Night of Four Years, Nicholas Pappas. Athens, 1946
Lyrical Life (volumes 1-2-3), Angelos Sikelianos. Athens, 1947

IN FRENCH:

Chants Populaires de la Grèce Moderne (two volumes), Claude Charles Fauriel. Paris, 1824-25
La Lyre, Andreas Calvos, odes traduites par Stan. Julien. Paris, 1824
Cours de Littérature Grecque Moderne, Neroulos Rhizos. Paris, 1828
Trois Poèmes Vulgaires, Theodore Prodromus, traduction française, E. Miller and E. Legrand. Paris, 1875.
Chansons Populaires Grecques, Emile Legrand. Paris, 1876
Morceaux Choisis en Grec savant de 19 siècle, Emile Legrand, Paris, 1903

La Grece Actuelle dans Ses-Poetes, Hubert Pernot. Paris, 1921

Histoire de la Litterature Grecque Moderne, traduite de Neerlandais par Hubert Pernot. Paris, 1924

Le Tombeau, Kostes Palamas, traduction par Pierre Baudry. Athens, 1930.

Choix de Poesies, Kostes Palamas, traduite par Pierre Baudry. Athens, 1930

Anthologie des Poetes Neo Grecs (1886-1929), traduite par Jean Michel. Paris, 1930.

Les Douzes Paroles de tsigane, Kostes Palamas, traduite par Eugene Clement. Paris, 1931

L'ARCHE. October, 1945

Poemes, Odysseus Elytis, texte avec traduction par Robert Levesque. Athens, 1945

Poemes, Georges Seferis, choix de poemes, traduits par Robert Levesque. Athens, 1945.

Poesie de la Grece Moderne, Samuel Baud Bovy. Paris, 1946

Le Serment sur le Styx, Angelos Sikelianos, traduite par Octave Merlier. Athens, 1946.

IN ENGLISH:

Modern Greek Literature, NORTH AMERICAN REVIEW. Boston, 1829

An Outline of the Literary History of Modern Greece, Alexander Negris. Edinburgh, 1833

Greek Literature, Richard Claverhouse Jebb. London, 1880

Modern Greece, Richard Claverhouse Jebb. London, 1880

A Hymn to Liberty, Dionysios Solomos, translated by Arnold Green, in *Greek and What Next?* Providence, 1884

Greece, Sir John Pentland Mahaffy. New York, 1892.

Excursions in Greece, Charles Diehl, translated by E. R. Perkins. 1893

A Survey of Greek Civilization, Sir John Pentland Mahaffy, Pa. 1896

Neohellenic Language and Literature, Platon Drakoules. Oxford, 1897

A History of Greece, Evelyn Abbott. New York, 1901

WORKS CONSULTED

A History of Greece, Charles Alan Fyffe. New York, 1902

The Rise of the Greek Epic, Gilbert Murray. Oxford, 1911

Life Immovable, Kostes Palamas, first part translated by Aristedes E. Phoutrides. Cambridge, Mass., 1919

A Hundred Voices and Other Poems, from the second part of *Life Immovable*, by Kostes Palamas, translated by Aristedes E. Phoutrides. Cambridge, Mass., 1919

Three Cretan Plays, translated from the Greek by F. H. Marshall. London, 1921

Greece, Old and New, Aristedes E. Phoutrides. New York, 1921

The Poetry of C. P. Cavafy, E. M. Forster, Pharos and Pharillon, Hogarth Press, 1923.

Greek Civilization and Character, Arnold J. Toynbee. London, 1924

Greek Life and Thought, Larue Van Hook. New York, 1924

Modern Greek Poems, selected and rendered into English by Theodore Ph. Stephanides and George C. Katsimbalis. London, 1926.

Palamas and the Western World, David Harrison Stevens in *Verses Mild and Harsh*. Chicago, 1928

Modern Greek Poetry and Kostes Palamas, by Sotiris Skipis in *Verses Mild and Harsh*. Chicago, 1928

The Erotokritos, John Mavrogordato. London, 1929

Verses Mild and Harsh, Kostes Palamas. Chicago, 1928

The Grave, Kostes Palamas, translated by Demetrius Michalaros. ATHENE, 1930

The Greek Way, Edith Hamilton. New York, 1930

Modern Greece, John Mavrogordato. London, 1931

The Customs and Lore of Modern Greece, Rennell Rodd Rennell. London, 1932

The Klephts in Modern Greek Poetry, Gabriel Rambotis. University of Chicago, 1932.

C. P. Cavafy, Dr. Raphael Demos, NEW REPUBLIC, New York, LXXVII (1933-34)

Hellas and Hellenism, Nicholas Panagis Vlachos. Boston, 1936.

A Greek Poet, George Seferis by Baud Bovy, THE LINK, London, 1938

Some Questions of the Psychology of the Modern Greeks, by George Theotokas, THE LINK. London, June 1938

Modern Versus Ancient Greek, Petros Vlastos, THE LINK. London, June 1938

Greek Art and Literature, Thomas B. Londsdale Webster. Oxford, 1939.

Paideia, Werner Wilhelm Jaeger, translated by G. Highet. New York, 1939

Cavafis, C. G. Tarelli, THE LINK. London, June 1939

Dionysios Solomos, Romilly Jenkins. Cambridge Univ. Press, 1940

Notes on the Byzantine Epic, Henri Gregoire, BYZANTION, V. 15. Boston, 1940-41

Modern Greek Studies and Materials in the United States, Peter Topping, BYZANTION, V. 15. Boston, 1940-41

Greek Literature Attains Its Majority, Michael Politis, BOOKS ABROAD, 1941

Modern Greek Literature, Michael Politis, AMERICANA

Palamas and Phoutrides, David M. Robinson. ATHENE, 1943

Life Immovable, Kostes Palamas. ATHENE, 1943

Life and Works of Kostes Palamas, Eugene Clement. ATHENE, 1943

The Twelve Lays of the Gypsy, an analysis of the poem by Theodore Ph. Stephanides and George C. Katsimbalis. ATHENE, 1943

The Great Age of Greek Literature, Edith Hamilton. N. Y., 1942

Greek Language, Carroll M. Brown, AMERICANA

Scope and Character of Greek Literature, Demetrius Michalaros. ATHENE, 1943

General Characteristics of Modern Greek Literature, Andre Mirabel. ATHENE, 1943

The Poetry of Medieval and Post-Byzantine Greece, Demetrius Michalaros. ATHENE, 1943

The Gigantic Sunrise, Henry Miller. ATHENE, 1943

Angelos Sikelianos, Eva Sikelianou. ATHENE, 1943

Erotokritos, Demetrius Michalaros. ATHENE, 1943

Solomos the Poet, Demetrius Michalaros. ATHENE, 1944

Kostas Krystallis, Demetrius Michalaros. ATHENE, 1944

Poems, by Joseph Eliyia, translated from the Greek by Rae Dalven. New York, 1944

An Introduction to Modern Greek Poetry, Demetrius Capetanakis, NEW WRITING AND DAYLIGHT, 1944

The Stygian Oath, by Angelos Sikelianos, translated from the Greek by Eva Sikelianos and Elsa Barker, AMERICAN SCHOLAR, New York, Autumn 1944

Akritan Songs, Angelos Sikelianos, translated from the Greek by Paul Nord. New York, 1944

The Path of the Great, Stephen Gargilis. Boston, Mass., 1945

A Greek Poet, Angelos Sikelianos, by Hero Pesopoulos, NEW WRITING AND DAYLIGHT, 1945

Zito Hellas, Cyril E. Robinson. London, 1946

HORIZON, A Review of Literature and Art. London, March, 1946

Marxism and Poetry, George Thomson, International Publishers. New York, 1947

Kostes Palamas, Romilly Jenkins. London, 1947

The King of Asine and Other Poems, by George Seferis, translated from the Greek by Nanos Valaoritis, Bernard Spencer, Lawrence Durrell. London, 1948

INDEX OF TITLES

Acheloos (The River-God), page 205
A Dead Maiden's Complaint, 112
Altar of Liberty, 274
Arise, beloved, let us go, 53
Athanase Diakos, 105
Athens (Kariotakis), 251
Athens (Rita Boumy Pappas), 282
Athens (Nicephorus Vrettakos), 295
Awaiting the Barbarians, 148
Battarias, 168
Body Remember, 157
Chess Knight, 279
Child of the Wind with the Harmonica, 292
Comrades in Death, 179
Daedalus in Crete, 222
Diakos, 253
Digenis, 50
Doomed, 225
Dynasty of Chimeras, 266

INDEX OF TITLES

Elegy on the Grave of a Small Fighter, 294
Epigram, 185
Epilogue, 261
Erotokritos, 59
For Ammonis Who Died at 29 at 610, 156
Four Years, 279
Girl from Roumely, 118
God Forsakes Anthony, 154
Granny Tassia, 234
Greek Earth, 141
Hands Thrust in Pockets, 260
Helen, 304
Hymn to Liberty, 85
Hymn to Passion, 134
Innocent Fears, 112
In Silence, 145
Ionian Song, 153
Ithaca, 152
It is Raining Again, 194
I Walked the Road of the Dawn, 184
I Would Love to Be a Shepherd, 160
Jesus, 264
Just One More Spring, 296
Kanaris, 119
Kyra Phrosini, 108
Kitsos, 52
Kleisoura, 212
Laborers, 134

INDEX OF TITLES

Lacrimae Rerum, 183
Lethe, 144
Let the Boat Go, 166
Letter from the Front, 209
Love Song, 276
Magic Refrains, 193
Manuel Komninos, 155
March of the Spirit, 216
Maria's Dream, 99
Maria's Prayer, 94
Marigo, 189
Marina of the Rocks, 306
Michael, 253
Militarism, 264
Morning Sea, 156
Mount Rhodope, 176
Noble Parentage, 147
Of the Ship, 158
Olive Tree, 145
One of the Jews (50 A.D.), 158
Only for this I grieve for you, 45
Our Torah, 263
Photinos, 103
Playing the Lyre, 192
Plebian Song, 235
Prayer to God, 248
Prevesa, 252
Resistance, 215

INDEX OF TITLES

Return, 154
Reveille for the Dead, 178
Rose-Fragrance, 122
Sad Sunsets, 188
Satrapy, 151
Serenade at the Window of the Wise Man, 187
Since Nine O'Clock, 157
Sinner, 246
Sleep, 250
Song to My Sister, 286
Spring, 68
Spring Storm, 170
Spring Symphony, 288
Sweet Athens, 199
Sweet Death, 146
Takis Plumis, 173
Temptation, 84
The Almond Tree, 142
The Ballad of Andrew, 228
The Bridge of Arta, 43
The Cistern, 255
The City, 149
The Clown, 260
The Creeping Vine, 109
The Cretan, 88
The Dead Youth, 133
The Death of the Klepht, 52
The Destruction of Psara, 84

The Dream (Solomos), 92
The Dream (Vizinos), 115
The Embroidery on the Kerchief, 164
The Execution of the Klepht, 101
The Fall of Constantinople, 51
The Fathers, 122
The Forest, 172
The "Good" People, 229
The Grave, 123
The Haunted Ship, 268
The Hidden Sorrow, 116
The Laborer, 247
The Last Fairy-Tale, 184
The Little Servant, 273
The Lover of His Country, 70
The Mad Pomegranate Tree, 303
The Mother of Christ, 226
The Ocean, 76
The Odyssey, 236
The Old Shepherd, 190
The Pains of the Virgin Mary, 229
The Prayer of the Humble, 186
The Sacred Way, 219
The Satyr or the Song of Nudity, 129
The Song of Freedom and the Sea, 284
The Song of the Vanquished, 195
The Spring Night (from), 114
The Stygian Oath, 206

INDEX OF TITLES

The Trip, 184
The Twelve Songs of the Gypsy, 124
The Village of Love, 181
The Vintage, 162
The Wedding Song, 48
The Witch's Daughter, 47
The Young Provincial, 270
33 Days, 297
To a Mother, 272
To Francesca Frazer, 85
To My Mother, 181
To the Imperial Eagle, 160
To the Sacred Battalion, 74
Trojans, 150
Two, 111
Vampire, 54
Vespers, 143
Very Seldom, 155
Vestal Virgins, 176
War Hymn, 65
Woman from Samos, 120
Walls, 150
Women of Suli, 201
You did not deserve it, 45
You Will Remember Me, 200

INDEX OF POETS

Anthias, Tefcros, *page 260*
Avgeris, Markos, *234*
Calvos, Andreas, *70*
Cavafy, C. P., *148*
Drossinis, Georgios, *141*
Eliyia, Joseph, *263*
Elytis, Odysseus, *303*
Emmanuel, Kassaris, *266*
Griparis, Yiannis, *176*
Hatzopoulos, Kostes, *166*
Kariotakis, Kostas, *250*
Karvounis, Nicholas, *195*
Kazantzakis, Galatea, *246*
Kazantzakis, Nicholas, *236*
Kornaros, Vincenzo, *59*
Krystallis, Kostas, *160*
Malakassis, Miltiades, *168*
Markoras, Gerasimos, *111*
Mavilis, Lorenzo, *144*
Melachrinos, Apostolos, *192*
Myrtiotissa, *201*
Ouranis, Kostas, *248*

Palamas, Kostes, *121*
Pallis, Alexandros, *118*
Papadaky, Sophia Mavroidi, *272*
Papandoniou, Zacharias, *186*
Pappas, Nicholas, *277*
Pappas, Rita Boumy, *282*
Pheraios, Rhigas, *65*
Porphyras, Lambros, *183*
Ritsos, Yiannis, *286*
Seferis, Georgios, *255*
Sikelianos, Angelos, *205*
Sphakianakis, Yiannis, *284*
Skipis, Sotiris, *199*
Solomos, Dionysios, *83*
Stasinopoulos, Michalis, *270*
Typaldos, Julius, *101*
Valaoritis, Aristotelis, *103*
Varnalis, Kostas, *224*
Vilaras, Yiannis, *68*
Vizinos, Georgios, *115*
Vlastos, Petros, *181*
Vrettakos, Nicephorus, *292*

JUN 26 '84 C

H54131

PA5289 $38.75
E6D3
1976   Dalven, Rae.
        Modern Greek poetry.

        1 5/91

Please Do Not Remove Card From Pocket

YOUR LIBRARY CARD

may be used at all library agencies. You are, of course, responsible for all materials checked out on it. As a courtesy to others please return materials promptly. A service charge is assessed for overdue materials.

The SAINT PAUL PUBLIC LIBRARY

DEMCO